Prayers from
a Seasoned Heart

Talking to God About
Life Beyond 50

Prayers from a Seasoned Heart

Talking to God About
Life Beyond 50

Joanne Ardolf Decker, Ph.D.

Resurrection Press
An Imprint of
CATHOLIC BOOK PUBLISHING CO.
Totowa • New Jersey

Dedication

To Jim,

with whom I share

the seasoning of my life.

First published in September 2001 by

Catholic Book Publishing/Resurrection Press

77 West End Road

Totowa, NJ 07512

Copyright © 2001 by Joanne Ardolf Decker, Ph.D

ISBN 1-878718-65-7

Library of Congress Catalog Card Number: 01-132740

Cover design and photo by John Murello

Printed in Canada

Contents

6   *Contents*

The Water Softener   72
The Amaryllis Bulb   74

SEASON OF LOVE

Beneath Mom's Quilt   78
Can't Sleep   80
Preparing for a Family Gathering   82
After a Family Gathering   84
The Little Ones   86
New Neighbors   88
Someone I Don't Like   90
A Stiff Neck   92
Misunderstood   94
Grudges   96
My Daily Walk   98
A Long Sleep   100
Death of a Celebrity   102
Visiting a Friend   104
Why?   106

SEASON OF CHANGE

Autumn Leaves   110
Mistakes   112
Traveling   114
Shopping   116
Getting Ready for Bed   118
Weak Hands   120
Seeing Well   122
Just One Today?   124
Background Music   126
After a Fall   128
X-Rays   130
A Close Call   132
Feeling Left Out   134
Feeling Invisible   136
Life Soup   138

Acknowledgements

I am deeply grateful to my loving husband, Jim, for his partnership in all my life adventures, including this book. His feedback, scripture searches, proofreading, and general support were key to my steady progress over many months of work. Three other good friends listened intently to numerous prayers, and I appreciate their affirmations along the way. Affectionately known as the Kuhn Sisters, they are: Sister Mary George Kuhn, SSND, Sister Daniella Kuhn, SSND, and Sister Alene Kuhn, SSND.

Many people—family, friends, relatives, and neighbors, inspired specific prayers, both directly and indirectly. A few that I want to mention are, family members: Sister Miriam Ardolf, OSB, Fr. Ed Ardolf, Dorothy Ardolf, Enrique and Janice Vazquez, Marco and Christina, Kurt and Sandy Jergens, Zachary, Adam and Mason, and my friends: M. Jean Wood, Sister Aletha Grewe, SSND, and Jan Huettl.

Emilie Cerar, my editor at Resurrection Press, was a tremendous support and strength throughout the course of these prayers becoming a book. She made the process a true joy, and I am grateful.

Most importantly, I want to acknowledge the Holy Spirit's work in my life and in this book. I am humbled and grateful to have these prayers make their way into the seasoning experiences of others. Thank you, Lord!

Foreword

In our "spiritual eldering" work, we speak of a person's age not as years old but as "years of life experience." Those years can be cause for celebration and the ground for harvesting the blessings and the wisdom of long-life experience. Or, they can be years of diminishment and anxious concern. In her prayers and reflections, Dr. Joanne Ardolf Decker shows how aging years can be a person's spiritual "bank account," with experience providing the "interest," the treasure to be discovered in the leisure moments of life's autumnal seasons.

Prayers from a Seasoned Heart sparkles with "life after 50" issues and insights that one can talk with God about. As the author shares her life experiences, she models well how her readers may harvest their own hard-won wisdom. Inspiration from the word of God and meditation on that word let the transcendent shine through everyday experiences.

"These prayers have been in the making for a long time," she writes. "Every so often, something would happen to remind me that aging was bringing changes to my life, and I was left to contemplate the certainty of getting older. . . . When I sat down and had a talk with God about it, I discovered inner strength that made me willing to find ways to cope with it."

Dr. Decker talks to God about the joys and sorrows of life, in addition to the changes of aging, gleaning insights and answers from the past, yielding rich meaning in the present. Her prayers express her spiritual intimacy with God. She remembers the past with gratefulness and looks to the future with hope and trust. Her questions—"more to pray about"— may encourage readers in their own meditation, journal writing, imaging exercises, and spiritual intimacy with God and others.

In our own ministry with and for elders, we are constantly impressed with the hunger for meaning in their lives, past and present, along with some apprehension about the future. Often they do not know how or where to find some relief for their nagging concerns, for some answers to the great questions of life. Prayers and reflections such as Dr. Decker's can help them with the issues that concern them.

Dr. Decker would feel right at home in our spiritual workshops in which we endeavor to create a caring and intimate community, where people can feel free to talk about their deepest needs. This kind of searching for meaning in one's later years is not easily found in a society that worships youth. Dr. Decker talks about her own search as she discusses a number of the needs of aging persons. Along with Henri Nouwen, we agree that when talking about our human and spiritual experiences, the most personal is also the most universal.

We have also found the wisdom of Formation Spirituality as presented by spiritual masters and writers Father Adrian van Kaam and Dr. Susan Muto to be a fruitful stream that contributes much to the fruition and harvest of the later years. Their emphasis on the "epiphanies" of everyday life and spirituality are echoed throughout Dr. Decker's reflections.

In our work at the Leighton Center for Senior Health and the Forever Learning Center in South Bend, we engage in exercises designed to "enable older people to become spiritually radiant, physically vital, and socially responsible elders." This is the goal set by Rabbi Zalman Schachter Shalomi of the Spiritual Eldering Institute and author of *From Age-ing to Sage-ing*, from which the inspiration for our work stems.

In journaling and dialogue encounters, in workshops and cel-ebration, we consider issues that can help people to change the face of their own aging "from age-ing to sage-ing." We ask, for example, to what extent have we unthinkingly accepted the images of aging proposed by our culture that supposes that peo-ple naturally slide into a weak and socially useless old age? Dr. Decker shows that, while she is concerned for her own aging gracefully, she is not caught up in the cult of the worship of youth.

We examine the cycles of our life, first maturity, middle age, and elderhood. Dr. Decker detects a larger pattern here, the com-pleting of the mosaic. She does her "life review" and her "life repair" with gratitude and forgiveness, noting the successes and failures of her life, events that can be re-framed and turned into opportunities for growth, and eventually harvested as a wonder-ful legacy for posterity.

In her reflections, Dr. Decker prays about her willingness to deal with life completion, of facing mortality in the increasing fatigue and medical tests, and a "body out of control," seeing in "winter beauty" not just another cold day, but "the sparkle and glory in every scene." She is allowing herself to be shaped into the beautiful person God has created her to be from all eternity.

She sums all this up in her reflection on Autumn Leaves. "It has taken me many seasons, books, and workshops to uncover the tone of my particular 'pallet,' the colors of my personality, the shades of who I am. I appreciate now how important it is to be myself, true to my own colors, as you made me, Lord."

We would do well to join Dr. Decker in learning more to be ourselves, true to our own "colors," as our Creator has had in mind for us from all eternity.

—Ken and Ellie Peters
The Sage-ing Center

Preface

These prayers have been in the making for a long time. Every so often, something would happen to remind me that aging was bringing changes to my life, and I was left to contemplate the certainty of getting older. When I had difficulty opening jars because my hands were growing weak, I was distressed at the loss of this simple skill, and I knew it was not likely to return. When I sat down and had a talk with God about it, I discovered inner strength that made me willing to find new ways to cope.

Similarly, when I came home dead tired from shopping, confused about what had happened to the "shopper" in me, I did a good deal of thinking about the situation. Again, I sat down and addressed my fears to God. I felt better. Such occasions repeated themselves over time. When I let scripture be my guide and addressed my fears to God, I felt better. Always, my heart swelled with feelings, and I found that when I expressed my concerns in reflective words, I gained insight and my faith grew. What began as private talks with God over my "seasoning" self, soon took the form of prayer.

Again and again, my awareness of life's changes led me to reflection. I'd sit at my keyboard and let my fingers type what was in my heart. I took my needs, complaints, and hopes to God. As time wore on, these little talks grew in number, and occasionally I'd share them with a few others who acknowledged similar occurrences and parallel feelings. To my amazement, what was terribly personal was by no means unique to me.

I realize that life's "seasoning" affects every one of us, and yet we can relate to each other's experience in spite of the individuality it takes in each life. Henri M. J. Nouwen in *Bread for the Journey* points out that "what is most personal is most universal." I believe that will be the case with *Prayers from a Seasoned Heart.* What I've said from my heart will strike familiar notes for others. The specific situations over which I reflected and prayed were springboards for my own talks with God, but I am sure that others feel and talk from a comparable heart. Although the circumstances and the words are uniquely mine, they have qualities common to others in the later seasons of life.

Nevertheless, I must admit that I am both grateful and terrified to share these personal reflections and prayers. I am most grateful for the Holy Spirit's work that brought these prayers into reality, but now others will know what I think and how I talk to God, and that is humbling indeed. I pray, however, that these prayers will lead others to reflect on their own life events, and that they, too, will be led to prayerful moments in deep relationship with the God who gives us countless opportunities to be "seasoned" in every season of life.

Because there are so many of us enjoying longer lives, we have a great deal to share with each other about the fears, joys, hopes, and dreams that surround our experiences with aging. I envision this book being a tool not only for personal reflection but for vibrant group discussions. The varied topics, reflections, prayers, and "more to pray about" questions offer abundant subject matter for discussion. I invite seasoned adults to openly address and share what is in our seasoned hearts. Let this book be a springboard for heart-to-heart talks among family, friends, relatives, and neighbors; in our homes, when we're out to lunch, on trips, in discussion groups, church groups, and during retreats. Let's not be afraid to "say it like it is" to God and to each other as we resolve to be fully alive after fifty and for seasons way beyond.

SEASON OF FAITH

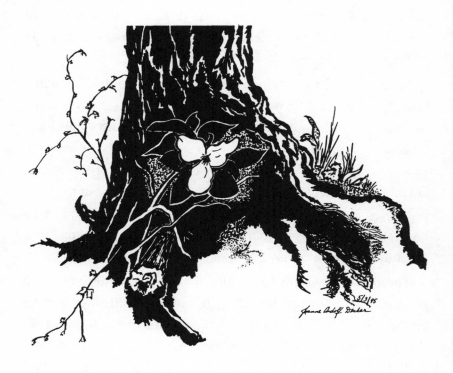

*"I see that I need greater faith to trust that you care
. . . for me and everyone—in every season."*

New Year's Day

*The Lord will be with you as you come and go, both now
and forever.*   Psalm 121:8

Happy New Year, My Lord! Wow! I wasn't sure I'd still be here for this one. But, sure enough, here I am. Thank you! As you know, I'm feeling pretty proud that I stayed awake long enough to welcome in the new year at midnight. As the years go by, my staying-awake power is waning, but I do enjoy TV's coverage of Times Square, and when the new year's ball drops, I stand up, do a little dance, and make at least a little noise.

I bring a variety of feelings to this new year, Lord. What will it bring? I have questions, expectations, hopes, and even some worries. I think about things like . . . on which days will I feel love? disappointment? friendship? vigor? illness? fatigue? generosity? forgiveness?—and various combinations of the above. On which days will I hear good news? bad news? about the birth of a baby? the death of a friend? an invitation to a party? plans for war or peace negotiations? about an overdraft in my bank account? or about my health?

The new year seems like a box of puzzle pieces crying to be put together. Unfortunately, though, there is no finished picture on the front of the box to follow. How will the pieces fit together? What will the picture be a year from now? If I'm still here, how will I look back on this year? Will I be proud of what I did? Will I have good memories? Will I consider myself better off? More importantly, will I be a better person? And most importantly, will

14

I celebrate that you were with me every minute, Lord, to quiet my questions and calm my concerns.

Prayer

Oh, Timeless God, with faith I enter this new year that you are giving me. I know that you are always at my side. Please guard and guide me to use this time for your glory, for the good of others, and for my own growth so that, indeed, I may grow to be a better person as the days go by. Help me to make good memories for myself and for the people you give me this year. And, just a reminder, Lord . . . I'd like to welcome in next year with my little dance, too. All according to your will, of course! Amen.

More to Pray About

A new year presents both endings and beginnings on which to reflect. Perhaps there are special matters I want to address in this new season ahead.

1. As I ponder the past year, for what am I grateful?

2. For what am I sorry?

3. As I look ahead to the new year, what hopes do I have?

4. Do I have some concerns?

5. Is there someone with whom I might share my aspirations for the upcoming year?

An Approaching Storm

The weather forecast is disturbing. A major storm is on the way, at least according to the weather experts. I tend to believe them. The clouds are looking ominous, the barometer is falling, and my arthritic thumbs have been hurting with extra zeal for the past several hours.

Oh, I know, a lot of folks would take those first two indications as valid. But my thumbs? Most would say, "Oh, really?" as they turn to roll their eyes and shrug off what I said. Well, perhaps they don't know their bodies well enough to use them to forecast the weather.

Lord, you and I know that my thumbs tell me a great deal about the weather, and I figure I'm entitled to the extra mileage I can get from putting up with the pain. As I see it, that's one of the benefits of being in a body for so many seasons – you get to know it pretty well, and you can make the most of both the good and the bad.

Oh, my! Here I am, Lord, bragging about predicting a storm to the very one who's in charge of storms. In fact, you're the one who calmed the stormy sea while riding in that little boat with your disciples. Now, that's quite a feat compared to a little forecasting! But you see, Lord, storms make me nervous. They are unpredictable, and I always feel fragile under raging clouds, in roaring winds, and heavy rains. They let me know who's in charge, and I know, for sure, it's not me! I realize, though, that it is precisely because you are in charge that I can feel calm and secure.

Prayer

In faith I come to you as the storm approaches, My Powerful God, asking that you quiet its fury and protect me from its rage. I give you all that I have and all those I love. Hide us in the shelter of your wings, as the psalmist says. You are the mighty one; the one who controls land, sea, and sky. I shall not be afraid. Calm my spirit, please, the way you quieted that stormy sea. I place my trust in you. Amen.

More to Pray About

As I recall storms – natural and figurative — that I lived through in my life, I feel gratitude for having managed through those times. I pray for trust in God's ongoing protection of me and those I love.

1. What natural storms do I remember? What figurative storms in my life come to mind as I pray this prayer?

2. What have I learned from the storms of my life – both the storms of nature and other "stormy" times?

3. Are there parts of my life that feel like they are in the midst of a storm right now? Is there someone who could help?

A Windy Day

And suddenly from heaven there came a sound like the
rush of a violent wind, and it filled the entire house where
they were sitting.   *Acts 2:2*

The windsock is whirling straight out there today, telling the
story of a vicious blast of air. Coming from the south, it's bringing warm air with it, so I should be pleased, I guess, but the
ferocious gusts leave me uneasy, Lord. I don't even want to go
out for my daily walk today. I know I will be hard-pressed
against the wind's mighty strength. I seem to have less and less
gusto to brave the gusts these days. I wish I could feel more
comfortable with the wind.

Perhaps you have something for me to learn from the
winds. Let me gain respect for the power of the wind, Lord.
When I hear its roar, remind me of the power of the Holy Spirit.
Let me imagine what your disciples must have felt when they
were overtaken by the Spirit on the first Pentecost. Nudge me
to let your Spirit overtake me and work your work in me.

Remind me, Lord, that not all winds are violent. I realize
that I am often unaware of the pleasant currents that drift
around me in nurturing ways. When I feel your gentle breezes,
remind me to thank you for the relief they regularly bring from
harsh heat and weariness. Let me recognize how you breathe
comfort into my life again and again without my being aware.
Yes, I trust that I can grow to love the wind, Lord. And as I do,

let me grow to love you more and more. "Oh, sweet wind, come and blow over me" (*Sweet Wind,* © 1994, Mercy/Vineyard Publishing).

Prayer

Oh, Lord of the Winds, let me feel comfortable not only with the winds you created, but with your movements in my life. Allow me to feel your power breathing into my very bones, and give me the faith I need to give you free reign, blowing as you will, to make me who you want me to be. Amen.

More to Pray About

God's movements in my life are sometimes like roaring winds, at other times like gentle breezes. The next time I go outdoors, I'll feel the wind and let it lead me to think about God's work in my life.

1. How have I felt God's work in my life?

2. When have I felt God's power in a swift way?

3. When have I felt gentle nudging from the Spirit?

4. With what kind of "wind" would I say God is working in my life right now?

My Face

"...And can any of you by worrying add a single hour to your span of life? If then you are not able to do so small a thing as that, why do you worry about the rest?"

Luke 12:25-26

Not bad. Not really bad. As I ponder my face in the mirror, I note that my laugh lines are prominent, but I like the evidence that I've done my share of laughing in the course of my lifetime. A few crow's feet to match the laugh lines. And, so what if my eye lids are a little puffy? I celebrate my eyes that can still see the puffiness! A few age spots add some character. Overall, it could be worse, Lord!

But then, there's this deep furrow right in the middle of my forehead. I remember that my first grade teacher warned me, already when I was six, "If you keep on frowning like that, the worry line in your forehead will make a deep groove that will stay all your life." Well, she was right! What an intense worry notch it is. It shows that I took things way too seriously over the years.

I realize that it's too late to make that groove go away, Lord, but maybe now I can use it as a reminder to turn things over to you rather than worry about them the way I've done too much of my life. And, what good did it do anyway? None, of course! Too bad I didn't wise up way back there in first grade and turn things over to you, even then. Is it that I want control? Don't I trust you? Do I think I can do better? Why is this so hard for me?

Prayer

Oh, My Considerate God, it is a never-ending challenge for me, this matter of turning things over to you and leaving my worry behind. I pray that I may be able to release my need for control and give the reins of my life to you. Give me the good sense to let go, Lord, and let you be in charge. Liberate me from worry, anxiety, and fear. Let me trust you enough to give you my life and my daily living but still accept myself as I am. And, I pray to accept my face—with this groove in my forehead and all. This is who I have been, and now I want to be all yours! Amen.

More to Pray About

Reflecting on my face in a mirror – what an opportunity for prayer (and perhaps a few smiles, too)!

1. What life stories do I see in my face?

2. Is there evidence of worry? Is there evidence of laughter? of trust? of compassion?

3. In spite of my faith, do I still give in to worry in my seasoned years?

4. How can I pray about my worry?

5. Are there others I know who worry and whom I might be able to help in some way?

Still Playing "Costume"

And why do you worry about clothing? Consider the lilies in the field, how they grow; they neither toil nor spin, yet I tell you, even Solomon in all his glory was not clothed like one of these.   Matthew 6:28.

What will it be . . . red blouse with black blazer? With or without scarf? The winter-green turtle neck with slacks? Navy jumper, silver jewelry, shiny rose blouse if it still fits! Oh! This is driving me crazy! At my age, still playing "costume" as my husband calls it (much like "dress up" for five-year-olds).

It's embarrassing, Lord, this stewing, fussing, and fretting about what to wear, and to just a little group gathering at that! Oh, I must stop spending waking time thinking about my outerwear. At least it's not my underwear! But, when it comes right down to it, Lord, I'll bet it's my inner wear that most interests you.

With or without an acceptable wardrobe, I suspect that when I meet you face to face, you won't be checking my accenting jewelry or the colors I coordinated that day. I have a notion that you don't pay much attention to the gear that I don each time I leave the house. Do you ever notice, Lord, just how well coordinated I can be when I set my mind to it? I'm sure I get myself in a tizzy over this stuff, and, here you are, trying to get my attention back to you and to the things that really matter.

Prayer

Oh, My Fashionable Lord, help me to worry less about getting all "gussied up" and worry more about becoming beautiful to the core. I need help to focus on my inner self and how to best tailor my individuality to fit you. I pray that you fashion my innermost spirit to match your presence so that I will, indeed, be beautiful in your sight. And, Lord, when I get into the habit of playing "costume," let the clothing I select remind me that my real goal in this world is to make you look good! Amen.

More to Pray About

What I do with my wardrobe offers opportunity for reflection. It, too, has many seasons.

1. Do I enjoy the process of getting ready to go out, or is it just a chore to complete?

2. Do I "fuss" over my clothing? Just enough? Too much?

3. What prayerful thoughts does my wardrobe lead me to?

4. Am I pleased with what I see in my closets? Are there things I need to add or delete?

My "Big" Mouth

If you know what to say, answer your neighbor; but if
not, put your hand over your mouth.   *Sirach 5:12*

You'd think by now I could take better charge of what I do and how I do it, wouldn't you, Lord? But, no! Again, I have come home, and I am scolding myself for saying something I wish I could take back. Oh, yes! I opened my mouth and inserted foot—for the ten millionth time in my life! Living longer is not helping me in this matter. What can I do to shift these ugly feelings of dislike for myself and find peace? I pray for some insight, Lord. Come quickly! I hate this state of mind.

Words are amazing. They flow from my thinking, come spewing out of my mouth for others to hear, and I can never take them back. Once they fly out, they are out. Now, all I can hope for is that the ears of those who could hear were busy hearing something else.

Maybe it's just my large ego that leads me to believe other people were actually listening to me in the first place. When I'm honest with myself, I must say that I don't remember everything that other people say, so why would anyone remember what I said? Am I just being hopeful here, Lord? Hoping beyond hope that my "goof" wasn't so bad after all? Well, I don't know how else to accept my foible, so maybe that rationalization is my saving grace. Keep me aware, Lord, that I am a work still in progress. So what if I'm not perfect? That makes me very human, the way you made me—incomplete, with blemishes that you will perfect only when I meet you.

Prayer

Oh, God of All the Right Words, I believe you love me unconditionally, even when I blurt out things I wish I left unsaid. I pray to love myself, too. As for now, I give you my self-incrimination and ask that you read it as my plea for wisdom. I believe you will make me wiser now, in the short run, to know when to speak and when to be still; and, eventually, in the long run, you will make me whole and free from imperfection. Oh, I know I'll have to wait a while for that, but I'm so very ready! Please give me patience with myself in the meantime. Amen

More to Pray About

Reprimanding myself in the midst of my imperfections can only make things worse. To truly believe that God loves me— no matter what—may be hard to believe, yet it is the key to accepting and loving my seasoning self.

1. What can I do to pick myself up and look forward rather than backward after a blunder?

2. Do I sometimes need to shut my scolding "inner" mouth and forgive myself?

3. Do I need to apologize or ask forgiveness for my outspokenness?

Having My Teeth Cleaned

Create in me a clean heart, O God, and put a new and right spirit within me.   Psalm 51:10

My dental hygienist is the best in the world, I say! She's friendly and caring, but best of all, she has a gentle touch in my mouth. She skillfully cleaned and polished my teeth today. Thank you, Lord, for sending her my way. With tiny, sharp tools, she delicately made her way around each tooth, scraping away plaque, stimulating gums, checking for problems. Finally, with a gritty polish and a slick flossing, she left me with a radiant smile. I am truly grateful!

Now, just imagine how thankful I would be if it were that easy to clean and polish my personality! That would be something, wouldn't it, Lord—if there were tools, (and they would have to be quite sharp, no doubt) to pick out of my character the flaws that tarnish my very self, detracting from my inner luster. What kind of picks or pliers could tweak out my whining, cynicism, conditional love, critical nature, grudges, or judgmental moods?

Would that a little grit and floss could scrub my roughness and smooth my inner surfaces to be more radiant, as you really want me to be, Dear Lord. I'll bet that's what aging is actually about. Yes, it's a slow polishing process! I think maybe that's it!

Prayer

My Loving Lord, I am beginning to see you as my all-compelling life hygienist. You are ever at work in my life, polishing away my pitfalls and stains to make me who you want me to be. Sometimes you are gentle in the process, sometimes not! I always prefer gentle, of course, but I realize that you may have to use more persuasive means to get my attention at times. Thank you, too, for letting my teeth last over these many years, Lord, so they could be cleaned today, and I could be led to have this talk with you! Amen.

More to Pray About

Although I seldom make a connection between my teeth and the spiritual matters of my life, even brushing my teeth may provide opportunity for reflection.

1. How does God work in my life to brush away or purify the recesses of my soul? of my personality?

2. Looking back on my life, where do I see that God used people and situations to rinse from me various tarnishing flaws?

3. Am I open to God's purifying ways in my life now?

Winter Beauty

I praise you, for I am fearfully and wonderfully made.
Wonderful are your works; that I know very well.

Psalm 139:14

What a gorgeous day, Lord! This winter wonderland is nearly more than I can take! The fuzzy frost on each twig and each blade of grass – well, who could do that but you. Oh, you are some artist! I praise you. I bless you. I sing of your goodness. Thank you for creating me and for sharing the beauty of your world with me.

To some, this might be considered just another cold day to get through. But my eyes see your sparkle and glory in every scene, Lord. Give me similar eyes to view the winter of my own life. I don't want to see my later years as just so many days to get through. Let me, instead, find delight in every day. I want to celebrate the many opportunities you give me to "come into my own." Let me put my unique twist on the colorful situations you give me and do my part to enhance the overall picture, even though we both know that you are the main artist here. I pray to be both creative and cooperative with your vision for my life. Today's radiant scenery is a good reminder of the endless possibilities!

Prayer

Oh, Maker of Magnificence, thank you for this lovely, frosty day! It makes me smile at you and at myself. When I think of how you can make such a beautiful day in winter, I am energized to think about what you might make of me in the winter of my life. Work your work in me so that I become a piece of beautiful art during this season of my life. Bring your paintbrush into my life with just the right tones, shades, shadows, and highlights to put a lovely finish on my days in this world. And, I surely could use the kind of eyes that see my frosty hair as lovely, too, – the way I see your frosty trees as splendid! Amen.

More to Pray About

God's beauty is everywhere if I let myself be aware and if I have the inner eye to see.

1. When I look out my window, what do I see that inspires me to give thanks to God for the wonders he has made?

2. When I consider my own life, what about me has become more beautiful through the years?

3. What are some specific gifts in my life for which I want to thank God now?

Medical Tests

For surely I know the plans I have for you, says the Lord, plans for your welfare and not for harm, to give you a future with hope.   *Jeremiah 29:11*

My body is out of control, Lord! It's doing things that I never felt before, things I don't recognize or understand. I've been to the doctor who seems just as puzzled as I am. Tests—we'll take several tests. No answers, just tests. I'm left bewildered and scared.

Dear Jesus My Healer, how I wish you were alive with us now, as you were 2000 years ago. I'd run out into the streets to find you and ask you to heal me, right there on the spot. I feel so much need for you now. I realize that my doctor is doing everything possible to solve my body's current mystery, but I feel terribly at risk, and with tests the only defense right now . . . well, I come running to you!

With faith I come to you, Oh Master of All Medicine. I place myself in your hands while I take my place in the arena of modern medicine. I trust, Lord, that you will guide the health professionals who strive to help me, to proceed along a path of sound inquiry, solutions, and decisions. Keep me cooperative, not fearful or aggressive; optimistic, not cynical or critical.

Prayer

Oh, My All-knowing Creator, you gave me my body as the temple of my life, yet right now I am experiencing it as a mystery with irregularities. You know what's going on with this body of mine. Please let my doctor and me find out, too. Work your work through the tools of our time — medical tests, medicines, and all such. I believe that you are no less active and loving than you were when you walked on earth in the flesh. I ask you for the miracles I need right now. I believe in you; I hope in you; I praise you; I love you. Amen.

More to Pray About

Surely I'm not the first person to feel alarmed about unexplained physical symptoms. I've known many people who are at the mercy of medical tests and doctors' decisions, but when it is actually me, it feels quite different.

1. Besides doctors and health professionals, who can I turn to at a time like this?

2. How can I pray myself through this critical time?

3. Is there someone else who is experiencing an alarming health condition whom I might be able to support?

4. How do I keep hope alive as I face the reality of physical diminishment as I grow older?

Severe Illness

For just as the sufferings of Christ are abundant for us, so also our consolation is abundant through Christ. If we are being afflicted, it is for your consolation and salvation; if we are being consoled, it is for your consolation, which you experience when you patiently endure the same sufferings that we are also suffering.

2 Corinthians 1:5-6

It seems to be everywhere, Lord – severe illness! And now my friend has been diagnosed with an advanced, rare, incurable type. I don't like those words. Any one of the words is bad enough, but the combination! Not good at all! I realize that we must have some reason to check out of this world and make it into the next, but somehow severe illnesses seem to be a cruel way to exit.

Hearing this news is difficult because I love my friend. Yet, when I'm most honest with myself, I realize that some of my distaste for this scene is my own fear of the same fate. What a selfish response, I know. But, you see, Lord, I know that something awaits me as well, something that will take my life from this body. When I face that reality, I know that I'm not so much afraid of dying, but I am afraid of the pain that's likely to accompany my lot. I am such a chicken when it comes to pain. And, the words "severe illness" always carry the certainty of pain in my mind. I know that's what I fear most.

Prayer

Oh, My God of All Love and Healing, I calmly pray for my friend who is ill, and for all those who are struggling with life-threatening conditions. I pray that they will have the strength to endure their difficulties, discomfort, and pain, and grow closer to you in the process. I ask, too, for my own strength to be of service to those in need, in any way I can. Teach me how to comfort others so that I can help to relieve their pain, even in small ways. Amen.

More to Pray About

People all around me are afflicted by a variety of struggles due to poor health. It is easy to focus on my own difficulties and miss the needs of others.

1. How can I help to ease the pain of someone else these days?

2. Is there someone for whom I can provide a bit of comfort?

3. Sometimes the family members of a sick person are also in need of consolation. Does anyone come to mind? How could I provide support?

A Friend's Funeral

For the trumpet will sound, and the dead will be raised imperishable, and we will be changed. For this perishable body must put on imperishability, and this mortal body must put on immortality.   *1 Corinthians 15:52-53*

Another one, Lord! I've lost another friend and helped lay her to rest today. Now I must adjust to life without her, too. It's becoming an all-too regular activity, Lord,—going to funerals! I would rather spend my time on other, more uplifting activities.

And this friend was so special to me. She had talents oozing from her, a personality like a magnet, sincerity I counted on, and we could laugh up a storm. There will be no true replacement for her. There'll just be another empty spot in my heart. Although I surrender her to you, Lord, giving her up is a tremendous sacrifice; but I guess you wanted her with you more than I can imagine. And why not—she's a gem, and now she can shine brightly in your presence.

Thank you for sharing this friend with me for a short time, My God. I recognize that my challenge now is to look forward to the day when I will see her again. What is especially marvelous to contemplate is that—at the same time—I will get to see you as well! Oh! What a grand time that will be!

Prayer

My God of Life and Death, I realize that I will continue to send you family and friends, one after another, until it is my turn. I pray to generously give them to you. This is not easy, Lord—this plan that you came up with! But I must say, it does work! Eventually, we all make our way back to you, where we can enjoy your love and each other without end. That does seem to be a fabulous plan in the long run! Give me faith and generosity to accept it, Lord. Amen.

More to Pray About

In spite of my faith, it is still difficult to give up loved ones in death. Mourning is especially hard work that takes its own course and its own good time.

1. For whom am I mourning at this time?

2. How did that person (or those persons) influence my life?

3. Are there other people in mourning these days whom I could help to console in any way?

A Barking Dog

Let the wise also hear and gain in learning. . .

Proverbs 1:5

I can't take it anymore! On and on that dog barks. It's early in the morning, and I still need more sleep, but no! Yap, Yap, Yap! What is wrong with her? She carries on as though someone cared about what's bugging her. But, you know, Lord? I don't really care, I just want her to be still. I like her when she's quiet, playful, and friendly. But this! Who can stand it?

Okay! Okay! There must be something to learn from this, Lord! Give me insight here—please—before I do something drastic to harm the poor dog! Is it that I should see how much I am like that yapping dog—whining and barking my head off about all sorts of things that bug me—the weather, food, what's on TV, bugs, dust that settles on my shelves! Oh, the list could get quite long, as you know! And then, of course, there's my own aging that I can always bark about. And now that I'm hearing this dog go on and on, I realize how little anyone else wants to hear it. Such noise is simply annoying! Generally, no one can change the things I grumble about anyway, so fussing only adds aggravation. Why can't I remember that?

Surely that's what I might learn from the neighborhood dog this morning! Right, Lord? It is a good lesson whether or not you had that in mind. Give me the good sense to quit my yapping about every little thing! Help me to stop annoying other people and focus on being playful and friendly—just like I prefer that dog to be. There's no doubt I'll get along much better that way, and, with an improved attitude, who knows! I just might have less to bark about and more to sing about.

Prayer

My Lord of the Morning, I am grateful for an early-in-the-day reminder that you have a lesson for me everywhere, and I thank you for that barking dog. I appreciate the attitude adjustment (at least for the moment) so I can sing your praises rather than bark out woes. And, sure enough! You have some sense of humor, Lord! I've just noticed that the dog stopped barking! Thank you for that and for this good talk. What a mind-blowing God you are! Amen.

More to Pray About

From time to time it is useful to reflect on my tendency to grumble and gripe. My own whining and complaining can make me quite like a barking dog to other people.

1. How does that image strike me?

2. How do I usually manage my exasperations?

3. Is there something I can do to generally have a more positive attitude and let go of negative things that happen?

Telemarketers

In my distress I called upon the Lord; to my God I cried for help. From his temple he heard my voice; my cry to him reached his ears.   Psalm 18:6

Help me, Lord! I may have made a mistake just now. My heart is pounding because I gave in to a telemarketer and agreed to purchase a "good deal" that might not be all it was cracked up to be. Her voice was assuring, the information seemed complete. I thought I asked all the right questions. I listened carefully to be sure everything sounded legitimate, and now I'm second guessing myself. Help me in my panic, My Loving God. I don't know where to turn except to you. Show me the way.

It's not easy—being alone yet trying to make the right decisions. I've never been the most astute about finances, but I keep learning, and I'm trying to do my best. I want to be a shrewd consumer. I strive to use my money wisely yet not be so penny-pinching that I never do anything adventurous. It seems more and more difficult to know what are good buys and what are scams. Right now, I pray that I haven't been "taken" by someone who is out to prey on easy victims. I don't want to be anyone's victim! Give me courage, Lord! Lead me in follow-up now, to calmly check out the company and the "good deal" and to find peace with my decision.

Prayer

Oh, My Lord of All Transactions, protect me from tricks and swindles. Give me sound judgment to make prudent choices —in every area of my life. Send your Spirit to guide and enlighten me in financial matters so that I act in my best interest—and yours too! I pray to make wise choices, and I ask for your ongoing guidance in these matters. Quiet my panic and let me be at peace in the midst of another opportunity to learn; and, please Lord, give me wisdom to act vigilantly, today and always. Amen.

More to Pray About

It is not unusual to feel vulnerable in the area of finances. Generally, it is good to watch for a bargain, but there is more to consider in a transaction than price. It is useful to review my methods in money matters from time to time with a wise and trusted person.

1. In what financial areas do I feel most insecure?

2. Who could I ask for advice if I need help with financial decisions?

3. How can I prepare myself for telemarketers so that I'm ready if and when I'm bombarded by their calls?

No Response on the Phone

Now the Lord came and stood there, calling as before,
"Samuel! Samuel!" And Samuel said, "Speak, for your
servant is listening."   *1 Samuel 3:10.*

Were you calling, Lord? The phone rang, I answered, and there was silence, yet I felt someone was there. Naturally, my mind spins after such an encounter. I begin to think I may have been hearing things. Some people think that's common among people who are aging, you know—hearing things that aren't there! No, I don't think that was my problem, at least this time.

Was it you? Was it someone who had something to say but couldn't blurt it out? Was it someone in pain or physical difficulty who could not get the words out? Was it an old friend who only wanted to hear my voice? (Perhaps I'm dreaming on that one!) Was someone too embarrassed to reveal an identity?

Worst of all, might it be someone who is checking to see if I am home, looking for just the right circumstances to do me some sort of harm? Such thoughts run rampant in my mind as I get on in years, less able to defend myself, feeling progressively more vulnerable. When I think about that, I quickly put myself in your hands, Lord, and try to let go of such useless worry.

Obviously, I don't like the kind of silence I found on the phone tonight. That is, unless I think that, indeed, it was you, Lord, just pulling me out of my stupor to get me talking to you again. The call led me to do that, I see. Therefore, it was the best phone call I've had all day.

Prayer

Oh Ever-present God, I believe you are with me at all times, whether or not I remain aware of that phenomenon. This silent phone call brought you to mind, so . . . you can call me like this anytime, to keep me mindful of your company. Besides, I know that one day, you will give me the most important call I will ever hear—the one that will let me discover your real voice—a sound I can only look forward to. Prepare me for that, Lord, so that when I hear it I will respond quickly and say, "Here I am, Lord, take me!" Amen.

More to Pray About

God uses many means to reach me in his daily-life conversations with me. Slowing down my life a bit may help me to be more in touch with God's actions on my behalf.

1. As I review the happenings of my recent days, is there evidence of God's efforts to reach me?

2. How have I felt God's presence in my life lately?

3. Am I comfortable with the idea that the events that occur in my life may be episodes of God's work?

Robins

*". . . Consider the ravens: they neither sow nor reap,
they have neither storehouse nor barn, and yet God
feeds them. Of how much more value you are than
birds!"*   Luke 12:24

Eight robins were in the yard today. Oh, what a beautiful sight! Thank you for them, Lord! Our lawn was just a stopping-off point, obviously, since they are gone today. They pecked the earth for worms, but the barely-thawed ground offered few. Will they find enough food, their destinations, their mates? I wonder where those eight friends-in-flight have been and where they are going. What was their winter like while I huddled under blankets on cold nights? And now, are they warm enough in today's slushy snow?

Oh, yes, that's right, Lord. You did remind us not to worry about such things, and you told us that the birds of the field do not sow nor reap nor gather into barns, yet you always provide for them. I see that I need greater faith to trust that you not only care for the birds but for me and for everyone—in every season! Anticipating spring is a good reminder to renew my faith, isn't it, Lord? I mean, right now I see only signs of new life, but the real spring is still coming. Just as I could see those robins as a message that spring is near, Lord, please give me eyes of faith to see the signs of you and your work in my life every day.

Prayer

Oh, My God of All Goodness and Care, I recognize that you are always at work in and around me. Help me to see that and not get stuck on the signs themselves. It is so easy to enjoy my life, my family, my activities, and forget that you are the provider of them all. But, these are just the signs of your goodness. Besides all this, I still have you and your living presence to look forward to. All this and heaven too! Give me the kind of faith that sees you at work in my life so that I can anticipate my eternal life with you. What a spring day that will be! Amen.

More to Pray About

There is great evidence of God's care for me in my daily life, but I must keep my spiritual eyes of faith open to see that wonder.

1. Does my faith help me to be aware of God's presence in my life on a daily basis?

2. What are some specific examples of the way God has provided for me and for those I love?

3. What signs of God's love are evident in my daily life now, in this season of my life?

SEASON OF HOPE

"I am delighted with hope in your plans for me."

My Birthday

For it was you who formed my inward parts; you knit me together in my mother's womb. . . . Your eyes beheld my unformed substance. In your book were written all the days that were formed for me, when none of them as yet existed.   Psalm 139:13,16

Thank you for my life, O Loving Creator! Today is my coming-into-this-world anniversary, and I am grateful for another one. My father used to say, "I want to have more birthdays . . . after all, when you consider the alternative . . ." and then we'd all laugh. But you know what, Lord? Today I want to consider that alternative, because when I do, I am filled with hope.

When I ponder the psalmist's words . . . about how you planned all my days for me before any existed . . . well, I'm overwhelmed with awe at your love for me; I am delighted with hope in your plans for me. Yes, this is a very good day to think about beginnings and endings; about both my life and my death; about seasons in this world and in the next.

As you know, Lord, on this birthday I find myself in a later season of life, but I am at peace, not fearful. I'm beginning to understand that the changes of my life are serving to bring me closer to you and to an everlasting season of glory. Although I can't begin to understand the alternative to this life, I place my hope in you that it will, indeed, be wonderful because you selected it for me—and for all of us. Thank you, Lord, for your plan of salvation that gives me hope today and every day!

Prayer

Oh, God of All Hope, thank you for another birthday and for this chance to ponder your loving plan for me and for all people— the alternative to this world—life in your presence forever. I love my life here, but I look forward to the next as well. While I'm here, though, I want to be a blessing to others and to do the work you have in mind for me. Let me use these seasons well in preparation for the one I'll share with you face to face. Amen.

More to Pray About

A birthday offers opportunity to reflect on hopes, dreams, plans, as well as on the past year and its outcomes.

1. What experiences of the past year are most memorable as I look back?

2. What events am I looking forward to in the year ahead?

3. As I reflect on this season of my life, what strikes me as important and worthy of my time and attention?

4. Are there particular people I want to make connections with? activities I want to accomplish? places I want to visit?

Tired of Winter

In peace and rest you shall be saved; in quietness and in
trust shall be your strength.   Isaiah 30:15

Don't you think we've had enough winter, Lord? Isn't it about time for a final thaw, more sunshine, showers, flowers, and all those things that make us want to sing and dance and shout your praises? Oh, I know, I'm whining! It just seems as though we've thoroughly done winter, and I'm ready for the next thing. Not yet? Well, then, open my eyes and my attitude, Lord, so that I can see some good in this long winter, in spite of my being tired of it.

I pray that I may appreciate these end-of-the-winter days. The stillness, maybe the quietness that is my strength! Winter is quieter than the other seasons. Hibernation is vital to the life of many animals and plants, perhaps to me as well! Teach me to be vitally quiet, Lord. Teach me how to use this time to restore and complete myself the way nature does. And, while you're at it, show me how to cherish my aging as an important phase of becoming complete. I am beginning to appreciate Eleanor Roosevelt's maxim: "Beautiful young people are accidents of nature, but beautiful old people are works of art."

Prayer

Oh, My Lord of All Seasons, I realize that in the winter of my life, it's not possible to ask for the springtime of my youth to return, the way we ask for the season of spring to return after winter. Not possible to start over, the way I'm asking for winter to be over and spring to come quickly. On the other hand, I'm sure that spring-time will truly come for me when my life here is over and I enter your kingdom where there will be a new life that I can't even begin to imagine. Help me to be ready, Lord, when that time comes. As ready as I am for spring flowers now! Amen.

More to Pray About

Quiet is essential to many aspects of my life and certainly for my spiritual growth and development. Even prayerfulness requires a certain quietude.

1. Am I comfortable with silence and being still?

2. Must I always be busy?

3. How can I grow in silence? quiet? trust?

4. What benefits might I reap from a bit more quiet in my life these days?

The Evening News

But this I call to mind, and therefore I have hope: The steadfast love of the Lord never ceases, his mercies never come to an end.　　　　*Lamentations 3:21-22*

Much to pray for! That's what I see when I watch the evening news, Lord. Sometimes I don't like to stay up to hear about the day's events because they give me a heavy heart. Too many hard-to-take stories about good people in painful life situations. But, when I look at the news as my prayer list, well, it is definitely something I must attend to.

It's only in recent years, Lord, that I am watching the news with that view. Most of my life I was just curious about novel, daily events. As I think back, I guess I didn't exactly identify with the people in the news. Although the "prayer list" approach is somewhat painful, I like this kind of eye for the news. I find myself more awake to your work in the world, Lord; more in touch with the daily joys and sufferings of real people. I like myself better when I stay connected to them through prayer.

So many to pray for tonight, Lord: people who are suffering the loss of their homes, children, parents, cars, health, self-esteem, politicians who think they know right answers, victims who have been abused, consumers who seek just the right items to find happiness, researchers who strive for cures, leaders who are making world-changing decisions . . . oh, such a bulging file!

Prayer

Oh, God of All, only you can give hope, bring comfort, supply strength, dispense justice, ease pain, and solve problems as needed. Show me how you might want me to help. Right now, I know that my part is to pray. Tonight I must sleep, but perhaps tomorrow you will let me know what else I can do. For now, though, I know you will be up all night anyway, so I give everything and everybody to you. Your love is all-encompassing. I realize you will lovingly care for everyone, in your own special way. I place my trust in you. Thank you, and good night, My All-caring God. Amen.

More to Pray About

The current local, regional, national, and world events provide more than enough matter for reflection and prayer.

1. Who are the people in today's news that I especially want to pray for?

2. Is there someone in a news story to whom I might send words of support? congratulations? condolence?

3. Is there an issue that I want to write about in a letter to the editor of my community or diocesan newspaper? or to a legislator?

My Computer

You saw my bones being formed as I took shape in my mother's body. When I was put together there, you saw my body as it was formed.   Psalm 139:15-16.

I love what this computer can do, Lord, although I have no idea how it works. It just does! That's as far as my mind goes. I have seen an amazing array of new-fangled things over the course of my many seasons. Even though I don't understand how most of them work, I still enjoy the results. I'm reminded of you, Lord, and how my wee mind can't fathom how you operate, but I'm spellbound by the results!

Although I'm just an amateur here at my computer, I still get a kick out of it. Last evening I installed a new operating system, and as I watched the installation process, the names of all the incoming programs flashed onto the screen, and I couldn't help but reflect on the operating system you gave to me and to every other living thing. What a vision that would be—if I could actually see all that you "installed" in me to make me who I am. Wow! Just living with all your gifts is amazing enough!

Oh, I know, I'm not exactly like this computer. It doesn't have free will. It is always conveniently in sync with the operating system I installed. I, on the other hand, can make moves contrary to the "system" you've established for me, and that is, of course, when I put myself in jeopardy of error. And, oh how I hate when "error" flashes on my screen. At least I know when

I heed your warnings, I am gently brought back to fullness of life.

Prayer

Oh, My God of All Operations, I pray that <u>you</u> will always be the operator of my life system. Help me to use the talents and abilities that you " installed" in me. I love my life and this world, and I thank you for keeping the world in working operation! Please keep me operating close to you—always. Amen.

More to Pray About

Over the course of my lifetime, many new inventions have changed the way we live. It is easy to take such things for granted; yet, I can find fruit for reflection in gadgets and devices around me.

1. What are some changes that I have seen over my lifetime?

2. Which "new things" most amaze me? Most confound me?

3. How do I usually approach new and innovative things? Am I open to them? Am I too frightened to try them?

4. Is there some "new thing" that I would like to try even though it intimidates me? If the answer is yes, how could I begin?

A Common Cold

My heart throbs, my strength fails me; I am weak and
faint.   *Psalm 38:7,8*

It's one of those sniffily, stuffy, sneezy colds, Lord. The kind that makes me feel like "crud" all over. It seems to be lasting forever, too, though the doctor gave me some medication.

As we all know, however, "It'll last two weeks with medication; about 14 days without!" So, I'll have to put in my time, no doubt.

On the other hand, I pray for quick healing. Lord. And now that I've said that, I realize what a weakling I am when it comes to suffering. All I have is a common cold—not some life-threatening disease, and I see that I'm pleading to be relieved of my distress. I'm totally second-rate when it comes to putting up with aches and pains. And then, to be so brazen as to ask for quick healing. Sorry, Lord! This is not my strong area, as you know.

There must be something for me to learn from this rather than simply ask for quick relief. I realize that just feeling ill has led me to come to you, Lord, so that is a plus already. Secondly, I recognize how dependent I am on my body and its proper working order. I am grateful for all the days of my life when my body functioned successfully without my awareness. Thirdly, a little pain is useful for me to prepare for any larger doses I may be called on to bear. Finally, I know that I'll be overjoyed to feel better when that moment comes. (And, of course, I'm ready any time, Lord!)

Prayer

My God of Good Health, with hope I come to you asking that you restore my health and energy. Today, with the psalmist, I feel that I am burning with fever, and my body is sore. In my weakness, I moan from the pain, but I believe you want me to feel good, not miserable. May I draw strength from you to bear with my current condition peacefully, without complaining. I want to keep my focus on you and grow closer to you through my discomfort. I realize that so many people are in the depths of pain today, far beyond a stuffy head. I pray for them and their quick healing. Amen.

More to Pray About

It is difficult to find benefits from aches and pains in my life, yet if I think about it and pray about it, pain does offer me important life lessons.

1. What have I learned because I've had the opportunity to suffer uncomfortable days over the years?

2. Is there anything I can do to resist disease and to recover more quickly?

3. Is there someone else who is in pain right now that I can help or pray for?

Going to the Doctor

Bless the Lord, oh my soul, and do not forget all his benefits — who forgives all your iniquity, who heals all your diseases.   *Psalm 103:2-3*

The day for my doctor's appointment has arrived, Lord. It seems this body requires more attention all the time. "One thing after another," as they say! Just getting to the doctor's office will be difficult, and then there's that long wait. Is it all in my head, or does it just seem as though they make people with gray hair wait longer? In my head, no doubt! Please straighten out my twisting thoughts, Lord.

Last time, when the nurse took my blood pressure, she didn't even look at me or say a word. I didn't feel very cared for. Help me, this time, to have the courage to start a conversation to set her at ease. Maybe she'll be more congenial this time.

Dear God, please give my doctor a compassionate attitude toward me today and the time to listen. I'm talking about the kind of listening you do. The kind that hears what I mean and not just what I say. Help me to do my part, too, by telling the important things in an understandable way. Then, Lord, help me to remember the directions, accept the outcomes of today's visit, and turn to you, My Ultimate Hope.

Prayer

Oh, My Compassionate God, please maintain my perspective today and keep my eyes on you as I venture off to this appoint-

ment. I know that earthly doctors and medical advances can help me, but I also need strong hope and relentless faith to focus on your long-range plan to restore my life for eternity. Although I am apprehensive about what I might hear from my doctor, I look to you for the ultimate good news about my life. I know that you love me, and you are with me today and always. My hope is in you. Thank you for your great kindness! Amen.

More to Pray About

My health is an ongoing concern and topic for reflection.

1. Do I have particular health concerns for which I need to seek help or advice?

2. When I request help from health professionals, do I do my part by asking my questions and voicing my concerns?

3. Is there someone besides my doctor who could be a good listener regarding my health concerns?

4. Are there other people whom I could support in the midst of their health problems?

My Big Feet

He drew me up from the desolate pit, out of the miry bog,
and set my feet upon a rock, making my steps secure.

Psalm 40:2

Big, bony, and "bunioned." That's how I describe my feet, Lord, but I still love them, and I thank you for them! They are big, though, and the way the bones stick up here and there guarantee that these feet won't be in any TV commercials! Worst of all is the huge bunion that bulges from the big toe of each foot. It could just be heredity, but some tell me that wearing tight shoes when I was young aggravated my bunions. And, it's true that I did smoosh these big feet into tight, high-heeled shoes, hoping such fashion would add to my beauty. It seems so silly now! Too bad I was so vain and overly concerned about looking just right. Now I pay the price with these bunions that permit me to wear only "granny" shoes.

That's okay with me, Lord! These days, I'm grateful to have feet and grateful to be able to find comfortable shoes for them so I can get around as I wish. What a gift that is – to still be able to walk and move somewhat freely, most of the time, without extreme pain. Plenty aches, of course, but not such extreme pain that I am immobilized. Thank you, Lord!

Prayer

Oh, My Lord of Sure Footings, you gave me two strong feet on which to plant myself, to firmly stabilize my physical being, and to move along in this world, ever on my way to you. Thank you for the wonderful places these feet have taken me, for all the dancing, hiking, and biking they did, for all the good people they took me to meet. Please forgive me, too, for the places I shouldn't have let them take me and for the people I ran with who were less than best for me. I look forward to the movement these feet will still provide me, and I pray that they will take me to do more good before my time comes to set my feet on you—my rock—for all eternity. Amen.

More to Pray About

Taking a good look at my feet may seem to be a silly exercise, yet my feet have been a vital part of my life and are worthy of reflection.

1. On most days, how do my feet feel?

2. Where are the strong parts and the weak parts of my feet?

3. For what activities am I grateful that my feet performed well over the years?

4. What can I do to take good care of my feet?

Fatigue

"Come to me all you who are weary and are carrying heavy burdens, and I will give you rest."

Matthew 11:28

How could I get this tired, Lord? I am completely "bushed!" It seems this kind of fatigue hits more often lately. In fact, I was so inspired by my exhaustion that I wrote this poem (and then I took a little nap!).

> Tired, blotchy brain.
> Thoughts stand still like pickled feet
> yearning to sit down.
> Groaning, sore, worn arms.
> Muscles, caked with ache, hang limp
> inside out, unglued.
> Slim sliced, squinting lids.
> Gritty eyes have seen too much.
> Pink, they shrink to close.
> Drunk with weariness,
> my skin cannot contain me.
> Body begs for rest.
> I give in.

How pitiful that I pity myself when I feel this tired. Poor me! I'm thinking, though, about how fortunate I am that I can go to bed, get some sleep, and for the most part, recuperate by morning. There are many people who are just as tired, maybe more so, who are unable to recover as quickly as I will from this siege of fatigue. A single parent, for instance, who has worked all day and must now care for a sick child all night; or, a doctor who has been called in for emergency surgery after a full day of seeing patients; or, a fearful child who cannot rest because of trouble in the household . . . Lord, you know them all! How selfish of me to think only of my own need for rest.

Prayer

Oh, Rejuvenating God, you are the source of all energy. I pray not only for my own rest, but I ask that you restore all those who desperately need new energy so they can do the things they must do, in spite of enormous fatigue. Give them clear thinking and careful moves so they can safely and successfully do what they must. Keep me tuned in to others who are in need. And, when we seem unable to stay awake one more moment, remind us of your words: "Come, follow me, and I will give you rest." Oh, yes, I look forward to resting with you! Amen.

More to Pray About

As my mother became more seasoned, I recall that she took many naps, and she often said, "I can do just about anything; it just takes me a long time!"

1. Under what conditions do I experience tremendous fatigue?

2. Is there something I can do to help someone who is extremely tired from his or her responsibilities?

A Strange Dream

He will not let your foot be moved; he who keeps you will
not slumber.   Psalm 121:3

Where does this stuff come from, Lord—these strange
images that are my dreams? As I was waking, people I don't
know were doing things I can't comprehend, wearing outfits
no one could imagine, in places I can't identify. Wow! I'm worn
out from this episode of mind jumbles! When I wake up like
this, Lord, I feel as though I'm in some exotic, alien place, all
alone.

Sometimes, my dreams are quite entertaining, but this one,
well, it was downright strange. Am I to find some meaning in
all this, Lord? Or, can I just think of it as a weird TV program
and turn it off, hoping never to see it again? Are my dreams a
means of touching another side of my mind? of another world?
of another me?

I wish I could understand my mind, with its many crevass-
es, powers and wonders. You made us with so much mystery
still to be explored, Lord. I'd like to think that by this time in
my life, I would be wise enough to understand at least myself.
But, no! Instead, the longer I live, the more I know that I don't
know much at all, especially about myself. My dream tonight
is another reminder of that.

Prayer

My Loving Lord, I come to you in a state of stupor, mystified by my dream, giving it to you. Maybe you will know what to do with it. Or, maybe nothing needs to be done with it at all. Who knows what this dream was really about. It doesn't matter. Through it all, you have been with me, protecting me. You never grow tired; your love for me is steady. Thank you! And thank you for this dream that led me to call on you again. Now, what do you say we just forget about it and have a good day together! Amen.

More to Pray About

My dreams leave me with much to contemplate. Some are pleasant, some frightening, some are simply strange. Writing down the dreams I want to remember may be both interesting and useful to me.

1. How do I usually feel after my dreams?

2. Are there some dreams I want to forget? Some I want to remember?

3. Is there someone with whom I want to share some of my dreams?

A Blue Moon

Praise him, sun and moon. Praise him, all you shining stars.   *Psalm 148:3*

It's a big, beautiful moon, the second one this month, and so they call it a blue moon. Therefore, this must be the time when all those unusual things will finally happen—those things that come just once in a blue moon! Wow! What a night this will be, Lord. Let me think about it . . .

Certain people are likely to show up and be in good humor; my favorite clothing will be on sale; politicians will make decisions based solely on the good of the people; shy lovers will reveal what is genuinely in their hearts; I'll win a prize; my cheese soufflé will be just perfect; workers will enjoy their work without stress; everyone will have a home; married couples will sit down and truly communicate; diverse communities will peacefully enjoy each other's company; all children will go to bed fed and loved . . . oh, what a fabulous list to think about! Yes, we need a blue moon more often, indeed!

As I age, Lord, I eagerly look for positive changes among us humans, the kind that show progress in our nature over the years. Before I die, I crave to see a shift from "blue-moon" human activity to standard best behavior on the part of us all. Oh, I know, Lord, this is my Pollyanna self talking. But, I pray that we become the best human beings we can be; and, surely this night of a blue moon is an appropriate time to pray this prayer.

Prayer

My God of Sun, Moon and Stars, I bring you this earth on which you shine your beautiful blue moon tonight. As you know, people speak of rare occurrences happening "once in a blue moon." So I dream, tonight, of wonderful, rare human moments that could possibly happen among us. Help us to be good people who reflect your light and love. Teach us all, as we live on this earth, to care for this world and live peacefully with each other always, especially tonight, under the beams of this lovely moon. Amen.

More to Pray About

A blue moon is a rare occurrence in itself, and it brings to mind the times when we speak of something happening only "once in a blue moon." It is interesting to reflect back to when I've heard myself or others use that term and consider the context in which it was used.

1. When can I spend a few minutes actually looking at the beauty of the moon?

2. What can I learn from the moon?

3. Just what would I wish for on a blue moon?

4. What positive changes can I realistically make or hope for?

5. How can I be a positive influence on someone or some situation today? this week? this month?

Trash and Treasure

Share with people who need food, clothing, and shelter.
Isaiah 58:7

Where did all this stuff come from, Lord? Surely no sane person would knowingly accumulate rarely-used goods and protect them in drawers and cupboards, years on end. Did I really do that? Amazing! What looks like junk today was a one-time treasure. And for certain, as soon as I throw something out, I'll be looking for it next week! I've heard it said that we tend to spend the first half of our lives accumulating things and the second half trying to get rid of them. Well, there's no doubt, Lord—I'm in the second half of my life!

Many things still look good, though. Like this apron that I haven't worn in years. I made it when I was a kid, and my mother saved it, so it tugs at my heartstrings. "Take it to a rummage sale," you say. But some total stranger, who doesn't know its heart connection, will buy and wear it. Does that seem right? How can I win, Lord, with such thinking as I pick up one item after another.

My life must grow larger than all this stuff! Give me courage, Lord, to discard what is junk and wisdom to share what still can be used. For instance, let me imagine the smile on someone's face when he or she puts on this apron to grill at a family picnic, showing off this pretty apron, and getting applause from guests. I would be proud to say that I made that apron years ago, and my mother saved it for just this occasion.

Prayer

Oh, God of All Goods and Goodness, I have confidence that with your help I will be able to clear out the stuffed corners of my world. I want to make room for you, my real treasure. Let me remember your warning not to store up treasures in this world; rather store up treasures in heaven. Keep me on track to save only what I need and to share what is beyond enough. And, I thank you for these and all your gifts—some of which look better than others right now! Amen.

More to Pray About

From time to time an evaluation of my possessions is useful. To clear out clutter takes courage and perseverance, but the result is worth the effort.

1. Are there things that I am storing for no good reason?

2. With whom could I share some of my things that I rarely use?

3. Would it be easier to sort through things if someone helped me? Who might be willing to do that?

A Bad Day

The Lord will keep you from all evil; he will keep your life.   Psalm 121:7

What a day, Lord! Right away as I reached for a cup, it slipped through my hands and shattered on the counter, pieces flying like darting diamonds. Thankfully, I had my slippers on so I could safely sweep and vacuum. That put me in a cleaning mode, so I started laundry and the machine stuck on rinse. An annoying alarm blared until I pulled the plug. Now, the repairman can't come until next week.

There was more! For tomorrow's group, I made a cake, stuck it in the oven, and while I fussed over laundry, it baked too long. Looking for consolation, I called my friend, but somehow she thought I was upset with her. Now I'm in trouble with my friend, too. I've had it!

I need to start this day anew, Lord! There must be something that can go right! Why is it—when things start going wrong, they add up like a jar full of jelly beans? It seems that I'm having more and more days like this, Lord. I look to you for hope!

Am I a spoiled brat who expects everything to be just as I want it, demand it? Am I ungrateful for what I do have, so I focus on what goes wrong? I'm not sure. Maybe it's none of these. Perhaps some days are like this and that's the end of it. Maybe some strange forces of nature are at work, and no one can change them. One thing is certain, though. These setbacks did bring me here to talk with you, so that's a positive outcome, right?

Prayer

Oh, Lord of All Forces, (even those that I don't understand!) give me the grace I need today to accept the silly things that mount up on the negative side of life. Help me to recall all the things that go right, especially when I take them so for granted. I know these are tiny setbacks in the range of possibilities, and I'm sorry to be acting like a spoiled child. I want, instead, to always be grateful for your innumerable gifts. Increase my tolerance for a little frustration, Lord. But do remember that I will be extremely grateful for a better day tomorrow. I will remain hopeful! Amen.

More to Pray About

Some days do seem to bring calamities from out of nowhere —and not only in our later seasons of life!

1. How do I cope with "bad days" when they turn up?

2. What can I learn from days like this?

3. Is there someone I can call on for a little understanding at such times?

4. Is there someone I can help who is having a "bad day?"

Feeling "Down"

. . . do not let your hands hang limp. The Lord, your God, is in your midst, a warrior who gives victory; he will rejoice over you with gladness, he will renew you in his love; he will exult over you with loud singing as on a day of festival.   *Zephaniah 3:16-17*

My heart aches inside me today, Lord. It feels like a rock that's pushing from the inside out, not like the soft muscle pumping life through my system that it actually is. Why does this heavy feeling come over me, paralyzing my thoughts and actions? As I review the past few days, I recall several things that didn't go well. Perhaps I let them accumulate into a huge snowball that rolled right in and froze my heart. Computer experts talk about downtime—when the computer isn't working right and shuts down. Well, that's what I'm feeling today— as though I'm not working quite right, and my systems have shut down.

When I feel this way, Lord, I know that the best thing to do is to come straight to you. You are the one who's able to take this weighed-down heart and perk it up with new life. Remind me of your healing love now—and always. Strengthen me to stop feeling sorry for myself, and help me to overlook the annoying things that shut me down. It's pretty egocentric, isn't it, to expect every day to suit me just right. Sorry!

Oh, Heart-warming God of Love, lighten my heavy heart! Give me the spunk to look forward, not backward. Lot's wife is a good reminder that looking back can be deadly. Oh! I don't want to turn into a pillar of salt, but I see that when I dwell on the past, I become immobilized. Direct me to move on, Lord, beyond petty things to more essential, heart-warming things.

Prayer

My Uplifting Lord, during this "downtime," my prayer is to forget the little things that led me to feel this way and, instead, keep a forward glance to tomorrow and, ultimately, to you. After all, this is just a temporary condition common to all of us in this world. Meanwhile, you have a permanent residence in store for me where there will be no "down" times nor will they be remembered. I look forward to being uplifted to you, My Loving God! And, by the way, I feel lighter just talking this out with you. Thank you! Amen.

More to Pray About

Feeling "down" is something that happens during every season of life, not only in seasoned years. What are some things that trigger my "down" times?

1. How can I pray my way through such times?

2. Is there someone who could help me at times like this?

3. Is there someone else I know who is feeling "down" right now—someone whom I could help?

The Water Softener

Here I am, awake during the middle of the night, Lord, and
the house noises seem very loud. Like the water softener running. I rarely hear it, but now that I'm awake, it seems downright noisy. It has several cycles, I notice, and they bubble and
gurgle in comical sequences. That machine is very busy doing
whatever it does, and I'm grateful for the comfortable-feeling
water that it produces.

It sets me thinking, Lord, about how convenient it would be
if there was some machine that would soften my heart—like a
water softener, but a heart softener! I need one of those every
once in a while. I wouldn't care how noisy it was; how much it
bubbled, gurgled, and bounced, if only it could get the job
done — making my heart softer, more gentle with myself and
others, more open to love, and change, and life.

Too often it is easy for me to be hard-hearted. I don't want
to be that way. My finest moments are not when I judge, test,
criticize, or fuss. I like myself better when I'm open, warm,
welcoming, and grateful. Yes, a heart-softener would be perfect! Just plug it in once or twice a week for more comfort and
ease in managing the matters of my heart.

Oh, I know I'm being silly, Lord, but it makes me think
about things, like how I can see you as the master "heart soft-

ener." I see that you use all sorts of life situations to soften my heart along the way. Lord, I want to age with a well-softened heart, resilient, adjustable, and pliable; a heart with spirit, zest, and substance. I know there is no machine that will provide that except the "machine of life" that you have set in place to jostle me around from time to time, to scour away, in various cycles, the hard crust of my humanity and soften me to be open to your ways.

Prayer

Oh, Great Softener of Human Hearts, I pray that I may allow you to do your work in me, so that I become soft and gentle of heart—the person you want me to be. And, Lord, please supply me with the grace I need to make it through the bubbles and gurgles and bounces. They usually feel rocky when they come, but help me to see their benefits and be open to the heart-softening times of my life. Amen.

More to Pray About

"Hard-hearted," "soft-hearted," "big-hearted," "gentle-hearted" . . .

1. Which of these terms seem to apply to me?

2. Are there some areas of life in which I am hard hearted?

3. What could help to soften my heart about those things?

4. How do I think others (family, friends, relatives, neighbors) would describe my heart—in the context of this prayer?

The Amaryllis Bulb

So neither the one who plants nor the one who waters is anything; but only God who gives the growth.

1 Corinthians 3:7

The amaryllis is blooming, finally! The sleek strong stem took its sweet time coming out of its bulb this time. Now there it is, both gangly and gorgeous. Four huge, white blooms sit atop the tall, green stem, nearly toppling plant and pot together. The stem proudly displays its top-heavy prize with sky-reaching confidence. And, why not? So much beauty to show, and such a short time to do it. As much as I love this blossom, I mind its short stay.

Thank you for this fabulous flower, Lord. What an amazing creature to contemplate. The bulb itself is a mystery. Round, earthy, stuck in the dirt, it sits and waits until, with a little water and light, some inner clock strikes, and the show begins. Tips of hopeful green slowly emerge; and then, with zest, the long stalk juts upward and eventually shoots out towering blossoms.

I feel like that bulb sometime, Lord—as though I'm still waiting for the right conditions to grow and blossom. Even though I have lived many years, I'm not sure that I produced anything significant. What do I have to show for myself? Have I flowered into something worthwhile? My time here is short, too. Well, it's a little longer than the amaryllis' life; yet I know that, regardless of how much time you give me, it will be too short.

Prayer

Oh, My Lord of All Beauty, this amaryllis offers splendor for reflection. Yet, all I want to do is enjoy it as an amazing flower that prompts my praise of you. And so may my life be—an amazing, unfolding mystery of praise. I leave it to you to decide how successfully I have blossomed along the way. I simply thank you, Lord, for letting me be a bulb of your beauty for a little while. You are the only one who can make me grow. Help me to "blossom" in the time I still have. Amen.

More to Pray About

Life is so very short, yet I want to make the most of it, whatever the number of years may be.

1. What do I still want to embrace in this world during the late seasons of my life?

2. Where can I go to truly smell some flowers and reflect on God's beauty everywhere, including the beauty God placed in me?

3. How can I share some of God's beauty with someone else?

SEASON OF LOVE

"I want to be a free-flowing person of love."

Beneath Mom's Quilt

I thank my God every time I remember you. . .
Philippians 1:3

As I lie here, Lord, in my warm nest of covers on a chilly night, I realize that this cozy cluster is topped off with the quilt Mom made many years ago. I'm pleased to still have it—not only for its warmth, but for the memories it brings. It lets me feel the warmth of Mom's love penetrating through the layers of fabric to my body and soul tonight. Her quilts were an important way for her to express her love. I am reminded of the poem I wrote about Mom's quilts some time ago.

> Quiet warmth
> under thick patches.
> Intricate, colorful show.
> Love woven. Time tested.
> Slumber comes easy deep below.

So I ask, Lord, that you let my eyes grow heavy with homey memories that leave me feeling snug, as though resting on Mother's lap long ago. Thank you for my mother and for her quilts and for all the things she did. I am grateful to have known the love of both Mom and Dad, and of my siblings, too. Through them all you let me have a glimpse of your great love, Lord, and how could I feel more comfort than that?

Prayer

Oh, My God of Ultimate Comfort, tonight I rest with my mem-ories and give thanks to you for the cocoon of love that I feel. Thank you for the people of my life who were instruments of love and good times. I pray that parents everywhere extend themselves in love and provide for the physical, emotional, and spiritual needs of their children. I plead that those who need love and warmth this night may find the support and comfort they need; and may we all come to know you and your tremendous love. Your gifts are so many! Thank you, and now good night, Lord. Amen.

More to Pray About

So many memories to reminisce with! The people who helped me make the moments count in life are rooted in my memories.

1. What are some of my fondest memories of my mother? of my father? of my siblings? of relatives? of friends?

2. What special items do I hold dear as remembrances of my family? of friends?

3. With whom can I share my precious stories of family and friends, and how might I preserve those memories and pass them on to other family members?

Can't Sleep

"It is the Lord who goes before you; he will not fail you
or forsake you. Do not fear or be dismayed."

Deuteronomy 31:8

Awake, for no apparent reason. I'm not ill, nor afraid, depressed, restless, nor having a nightmare. Yet, I can't sleep, so it must be that you want to chat, Lord. That's fine. Actually, I've come to appreciate my middle-of-the-night visits with you. You always seem to have something extra special to say at these times. So, I'll go sit in my favorite chair, and we can visit.

I love to be here with you, just being in your presence, My Loving God. You seem profoundly near in the middle of the night, as though I can sit on your lap and breathe in life from your essence. You are so very close. Or, is it that I am more near to you?

I'll just be quiet for awhile and let you talk. We don't need to say much. You already know all that's on my mind and in my heart. You know all those I love and how I want to pray for them. You know all my concerns and how I give them to you, to have you care for them. I believe that you will look after all that is in my heart. I give it to you and entrust it to your deep wisdom and love.

Prayer

Oh, Gentle God, your presence is ever-so warm and tender as I
sit here with you now. Thank you for all the gifts you grant me and

for the many ways you show yourself to me. I know that you are always with me, constantly bringing me back to you no matter how far from you I wander. Thank you for diligently pursuing me in your love. I pray that I may always be willing to be found. You are ever with me; you will never forsake me. And, thank you for getting me up for this special time with you tonight, Lord. I feel myself nodding off, so I'll go back to bed to finish my sleep. I love you, and good night – again! Amen.

More to Pray About

Sleep does not always begin and end on the time schedule I have in mind. Lying awake can provide an opportunity to pray and reflect. Sometimes getting up to "sit with" God for awhile can bring great comfort.

1. Under what circumstances do I find myself awake at night?

2. When I lie awake, do I easily become frustrated?

3. Can I comfortably bask in my awareness of God's presence?

4. What can I do to make my night "awake" times into valuable moments?

Preparing for a Family Gathering

She rises early to prepare food for her family and plans
for what others should do.   Proverbs 31:15

A family gathering is coming up, Lord, and I am "in charge" of the party. It seems that the food, decorations, and activities are the easy part. Communicating with everyone, now that's another thing! It's taking huge amounts of energy to bring our small family into the same place at the same time to celebrate something special. The phone calls, e-mail messages, and reminder notes seem endless right now.

Oh, don't get me wrong. I love our gatherings, and I rather enjoy planning what foods to have, preparing some of it, and giving "orders" about who should bring what. I get a kick out of creating decorations, and I even relish thinking up activities that will keep kids content and safe while adults chat among themselves. But now that my family members have their own families, the dynamics among us are remarkable when we come together, quite something to experience!

There's no way to thoroughly plan around all the eventualities. At any given time, each family is encountering something different, and within each family are mini-crises, immediate wants, rightful demands for attention, help, care, and concern. It's hard to know what will happen when we become a "bunch." Surely this is a good time to "let go and let God" as they say!

Prayer

As always, My Loving God, I come to you, bringing with me this "lovely bunch of coconuts" that is my family. I love them all, individually and jointly, and I bring us all to you just as we are. I pray for a few clues, though, so I can help to meet the needs of even some while we're together. Bless us in our sameness and in our differences, and make of us a rich blend of love and friendship. Most importantly, Lord, I pray that one day we will all be together in heaven with you where we can be your family forever. Oh, will we celebrate then! Amen.

More to Pray About

Every family is different from every other family in the ways they relate and celebrate. Taking time to reflect on my own family and our get-togethers can be entertaining, and perhaps, motivation for prayer!

1. As I reflect on most of our family gatherings, what strikes me as particularly unique about my family?

2. What usually goes very well when we celebrate together?

3. What goes least well?

4. How can I simplify preparations so that I don't overextend my energies?

5. When I have family concerns, with whom can I talk openly and honestly?

After a Family Gathering

You will be blessed with happiness and the fruit of your
labor.   Psalm 128:2

Ah, we did it, Lord! We managed to come together, celebrate as a family, have a relatively (no pun intended!) good time, and get everyone back home safely. The party turned out fine. Actually, it turned into a memorable family event, and I am deeply grateful. Of course, I feel more tired than I've felt in many a day—ready to collapse—but what a good cause! I'll just take a few more naps this week to recover.

As I roll the day through my mind, I realize that it was indeed festive. Everyone arrived with an air of expectation, so I knew right away that we were off to a good start. The food was good; the decorations mostly stayed up; the kids played together without permanently harming each other; and adults chatted together in good humor. What more could I ask?

But my favorite part of the day was the program! Thank you, Lord, for inspiring me some days before, to call everyone and mention that it might be fun to have a little family talent show as part of our celebration. I was amazed at the way everyone picked up this idea and came through with unique contributions. It felt great, Lord, to look around and see us singing somewhat in harmony, laughing together at lip-sync acts, skits, jokes, and little kids' dances. Thank you for the talents you gave to each of us, Lord. We are quite a unique batch of humanity. Thank you, too, for giving us a sharing spirit so we could lose ourselves in fun and unity.

Prayer

Oh, Lord of All Families, I thank you for mine. We are far from a story-book-sort-of family, but we have our good points, and best of all, we do love each other. Not that it's always evident, I know, but our love is genuine, and we know we can count on each other, no matter what. You were generous to provide me with these people to be my family. I pray that we will always be close and that we will lead each other ever closer to you. Dear God, bless us—one and all! And bless, too, those people who do not have family with whom they can share special times. Please give them the support of others who can serve as family in the absence of the real thing. Amen.

More to Pray About

Family photos, journaling, scrapbooks, letters of thanks, are all ways to treasure special family moments.

1. Do I make a point of relishing our good times?

2. What can I do to improve our get-togethers? to improve the follow-up?

3. Although I enjoy family gatherings, sometimes I am very tired afterward; what can I do—before, during, after—to ease my fatigue?

The Little Ones

"Truly I tell you, whoever does not receive the kingdom
of God as a little child will never enter it." Luke 18:17

What a great day, Lord! I played paper dolls, cards, board games, hide-and-seek, ball games, had a tea party, and read a few stories. Exhaustion reigns now, but I'll recover! My playmates? The little ones of the family, and we had a hilarious time. Thank you for the children in my life! They make me giggle and beam, and they let me be three, five, seven, or nine—depending on the game and who's playing. Their authentic selves are full of surprises, and they teach me a great deal. I love to see how they solve problems, learn, remember, laugh, compete, demand attention, imagine, pretend, strategize, and take leads from me, too.

Often, in the midst of activity, I enjoy slipping in my own little twists: a before-tea-party prayer, minor treatises on playing fair, speaking one-at-a-time, what Jesus would do, and such. The kids seem to know that, when I'm in the group, there'll be a "lesson" here and there. Seems they don't mind, and we have fun just the same.

No doubt you play in my life that way, too, Lord, letting me immerse myself in my life games of family, work, community, friends, and so on, while you slip in lessons for me to learn. What a clever Father you are! You are always there, part of it all, steering, guiding, teaching; and, we have fun just the same!

Prayer

Oh, Loving Father, thank you for putting children in my life to add sparkle to my days. They are a blessing to me! I pray for the gift of being child-like. Let me learn from the children in my family, to be playful and genuine yet open to the life lessons you want me to learn, even now, in the late seasons of my life. You said that we must accept your kingdom as a little child. I pray for the children of my family and for their parents, and all parents, to be loving models of God-centered living. May we all grow in child-like traits, understand your ways, and eventually come to live with you as one family—as your children—forevermore. Amen.

More to Pray About

Children can be a wonderful balancing force in my life; yet, they require a good deal of time and energy, too. In later years, children may not be as available as earlier in life, especially if family members live at a distance.

1. Who are the children in my life these days and how do I relate to them? What brings me joy? What causes frustration?

2. If children of the family are not nearby, what other children might I enjoy . . . in the neighborhood? at church? through volunteer activity?

3. What lessons could I learn from being around children these days?

New Neighbors

Another change in the neighborhood, Lord! New folks are moving in down the way. I can watch the action from my window and wonder. Who are they? How many are there? Do they have pets? Will they be easy to get to know? Will they like me? Will we become friends? Oh, how I pray that we won't become enemies!

I'll miss the folks who moved away. Now, these new neighbors won't even know about the good times we had in their house when it was the home of our old friends—how we grilled chicken on their deck, played cards at the kitchen table, roasted marshmallows in the fireplace, and swapped gardening tips in the back yard. I miss those good times and the good people.

Lord, I ask for wisdom now in this new relationship. Keep me from bringing up my memories of the past; and, instead, let me strive to make new memories with these new folks. Keep me, too, from expecting them to take the place of the former neighbors. I want to be open to a new adventure here. Yet, I must admit, that I want good neighbors to enjoy and count on if I have some needs. I realize that is a selfish way to think about them, but even the Book of Proverbs suggests that nearby neighbors are good substitutes for faraway family.

Prayer

Oh, Master of All Neighborhoods, you asked us to love our neighbors as ourselves. I will truly try to do that. Show me creative ways to get to know my neighbors as they are, and make me open to letting them know the real me. And, if it happens that we just don't "click," let me accept that, too. When I think about it, though, I realize that my best prayer for my neighbors is to ask your help in being a good neighbor. Yes! That's the focus I need. Teach me how to be the best neighbor I can be! Lead me and guide me, Lord. Amen.

More to Pray About

Some neighbors are more attractive to me than others, yet I may be able to cultivate true friendships among many neighbors.

1. What are some specific things I might do to nurture my relationship with neighbors?

2. Is there one neighbor that I would like to get to know better? How could I do that?

3. What could I do to "break the ice" with neighbors I don't know very well?

Someone I Don't Like

See what love the Father has given us, that we should be called children of God; and that is what we are.

1 John 3:1

I'm embarrassed to say it to you, Lord, but I will, because I need some help here—again! I just don't like her! Okay. There. I said it. I'm not very proud of myself, that's for sure. She grates on me, that's all there is to it. Why can't I change these lousy feelings? I feel as though I'm still in third grade, seeking the teacher's attention and disliking the kid in class who's the apple of the teacher's eye. And here I am, a gray-haired, seasoned adult who can't rid herself of such ugly feelings. Oh, my! I need considerable help, Lord!

I keep thinking of something my mother told me when I was a child. She said that it's more important to love a person than to like him or her. Mom said it wasn't necessary to like everyone, but that, deep down in my heart, I must wish everyone well and, therefore, love them. That idea made me feel better then, and it makes sense to me now.

I can wish this person well, Lord. My heart seems to be in the right place for that. It's just my feelings that are out of control. I look at her, and I know that, basically, she and I are very much alike. That must be why she grinds on me so much. All those qualities that I dislike in her are right here in me. I know that, Lord. Maybe you thought I didn't get it, but I do. I can even admit it, but I still feel helpless to change the feelings of dislike.

Prayer

Oh, My Amiable God, grow my heart to love and accept all your children. Please swell my heart to love the way you love—without conditions. Please share with me your generous view of human beings, including those that I find difficult to like. Let me see this particular person the way you see her—one of your children to love. Teach me to like myself, too, Lord. That way, since she and I are so much alike, it should be easier to like her. I promise to keep working on it, Lord, with your help, of course! Amen.

More to Pray About

My seasoned years are not the only times of my life when I've had the problem of disliking someone.

1. How has "dislike" affected my life?

2. Is there a specific person for whom I need to pray this prayer now?

3. Is there someone to pray for because I feel that person dislikes me?

4. Is there something I can do to change that dislike, or is it simply something to accept and pray about?

A Stiff Neck

He said, "If now I have found favor in your sight, O Lord, I pray, let the Lord go with us. Although this is a stiff-necked people, pardon our iniquity and our sin, and take us for your inheritance."   *Exodus 34:9*

I have a pain in the neck today, Lord, and it is giving me a twang of pain with every twist and turn. It's limiting my freedom, encasing me in my own body's traction machine. Where did this stiff neck come from? Is it another "something" that comes in later seasons of life? Is there something to value here in spite of this inconvenience?

Today's pain in the neck makes me aware of how I've taken for granted the freedom of movement that I enjoyed so much of my life. Most days I didn't give a thought to coming and going quickly, as I pleased. More recently, though, you are reminding me, Lord, that things are changing in this body. I notice that I move more slowly, deliberately, carefully. That's all right, but I miss my bouncing-around days when my body moved according to my every whim. I see yet another challenge—to get along well with this new arrangement, Lord.

Furthermore, this stiff neck makes me wonder. . . how often have I been a pain in the neck to others? Oh, I hate to admit it, but I know for certain that I've made at least a few of my marks in this world on—or in—the necks of other people. I'm sorry for that, Lord, and I ask pardon from you and send love and healing to those whom I may have hurt.

Prayer

Oh, Lord of All Cures, I come to you in my contorted condition, asking you to heal my stiff neck today. Please unlock my stubborn muscles and free my movements so I can resume me daily life. I also come to you pleading for healing among those for whom I have been a pain in the neck – at one time or another. Replace my stiff muscles and stubborn personality with love that brings new freedom to my life. I don't want to be a stiff-necked person in any way. Rather, I want to be a free-flowing person of love. Teach me how to do that. I ask you to receive me as your own! Thank you, My Loving God. Amen.

More to Pray About

Stiff-necked, stubborn, rigid, obstinate, inflexible . . . flexible, compassionate, kind, considerate, empathetic . . . an interesting array of words that may or may not apply to me.

1. Do any of these words apply to my personality in this season of my life?

2. How can I grow in the characteristics that I want to have?

3. Did I hurt people in the past because of my stubbornness? Who? What can I do to reverse the results of my stiff-necked ways?

Misunderstood

Then Jesus said, "Forgive them Father, they do not know
what they are doing."   Luke 23:34

I'm in a pickle, Dear God. I just got a call from a friend who
said she heard I said something that I never said. Or, at least I
didn't mean it the way it was heard. What a mess!

This reminds me of the little game we used to play in grade
school called "Telephone." Remember, Lord? We'd line ourselves
up, ear to ear, and the leader would whisper something to the
one next to her who repeated it to the next and so on down the
line until the last person said out loud what she heard. Well, it
was always a far cry from the beginning message, and we'd all
laugh heartily.

Now, here I am, decades later, and I still feel as though I'm
playing that game in life. But right now, I'm not laughing. Things
never change, do they, Lord. Age doesn't really improve certain
things. People are people, no matter how young or old we are.
But this hurts, and I know it'll take time and energy to set things
straight. Please help me with this, Lord.

Such confusion makes me think about you and how much
you are misunderstood. People are always attributing something
to you that has been misinterpreted. Mine is just a small matter,
yet I have deep feelings about it. But, when you were on earth,
Dear Jesus, how greatly you were misunderstood, in spite of all
the good you did. Now that was misunderstanding! Help me to

remember how forgiving you were! Let me keep you in mind, as my example, when I relate to those who have misrepresented me. I pray for an open, forgiving heart.

Prayer

My Dear Understanding God, I thank you for always knowing me, inside and out. I am sure of your constant understanding, whether or not others get things straight. Lead me to be comfortable with misunderstandings, knowing they are just part of the human condition. May I always remember that being understood by you is all that matters in the long run. And, please help me to accept this particular mess, and show me how to correct it. Amen.

More to Pray About

Since human communication is imperfect, even at its best, I must expect that misunderstandings will be part of my life from time to time. They occur in every season of life.

1. Are there certain people or situations that seem to generate misunderstandings for me more than others?

2. How do I usually work my way through misunderstandings?

3. Can I remain calm and positive during my efforts to correct things?

4. Is there a current misunderstanding I need to rectify?

Grudges

Bear with one another and, if anyone has a complaint against another, forgive each other; just as the Lord has forgiven you.   *Colossians 3:13*

I wish I could get rid of the silly things I keep remembering and hanging on to, Lord. At this point in my life, it seems important to be free from a troubled heart, and grudges that hang on surely are trouble for any heart. Yet, I find myself dwelling on things like: she never sends me a birthday card; he doesn't say "hello" when I meet him in the store; she gave away the special beads I gave her; he called me names when we were in grade school . . . and all such ridiculous stuff! Why do I hang on to grudges? Is it in our human nature to do that, or is it a weakness that specifically ensnares my personality?

No matter how long I live, Lord, this weakness hangs on. It led me to write this poem about a grudge some time ago, in hopes of becoming a bit sweeter!

The private smudge
that will not budge!
It steeps its sludge
inside of me,
then makes me trudge.

If I could nudge
away the drudge
of being judge
I'd sweeter be . . .
perhaps like fudge!

Prayer

Oh, My All Forgiving God, I pray for a loving, forgiving heart, free from grudges. Forgiving is terribly hard work, and I feel too weak to accomplish it. Only your grace can pull me out of the mire of my conditional love that continues to hamper genuine love. I ask that you teach me your constant, forgiving ways. I want to learn how to forgive everyone and everything. Please replace my grudging personality with kindness of mind and heart– soon, please! Amen.

More to Pray About

Grudges seem to seize human relationships in every season of life. Forgiving others is a very important gift that I give to myself!

1. When I'm truly honest with myself, can I admit to grudges lurking in my heart?

2. Is there someone from whom I am withholding forgiveness, thinking they deserve to be held guilty?

3. How do I pray about my need to be a forgiving person?

4. Can I forgive myself as well as others?

My Daily Walk

He has told you, O mortal, what is good; and what does the Lord require of you but to do justice, and to love kindness, and to walk humbly with your God?

Micah 6:8

Walkin', talkin', and gawkin'! That about sums up my daily exercise, Lord. Wouldn't you agree? Oh, I enjoy my walking time, and I'm grateful that I still can walk my mile or two each day. I feel much better when I get out and about. That keeps me just a little brighter, lighter, and spriter, as I say.

And, I enjoy talking with you while I walk, Lord. That's just as important to me as putting one foot in front of the other. I don't know why, but there's something special about the way we talk when I'm doing my walk. I appreciate time to tell you what's on my mind, let you in on how I'm feeling, and sometimes even give you a piece of my mind. Of course, I give you plenty of time to do the same with me. We have quite a good time of it!

And, now that I'm thinking about it, I believe that gawking is an important part of my walking and talking with you, Lord. As you know, I love to look around and check out all the beauty that I can take in along the way. That gives us plenty to talk about, too! Your beauty is everywhere, every day. The changes that come with the seasons, the clouds, birds, colorful skies, budding trees, flowering bushes, and all such. Well, it's never dull, and I love to feast my eyes as we walk and talk.

Prayer

Thank you, oh Lord of My Wandering. Be with me wherever I walk in your world. Please stay especially close so that we can talk along the way. And, I ask for keen eyes to see your beauty wherever I go. Always be with me, Lord—just walkin', talkin', and gawkin'—having a good time as we step through the seasons of my life. Thank you! Amen.

More to Pray About

Every day I need some exercise. Walking is a great way to stay fit, and I can do it at my own pace, going just as far and as long as feels good. Being outside gives me a chance to be closer to nature, too.

1. What are my favorite ways to be active and get some exercise?

2. What bits of beauty do I find when I walk?

3. Does praying fit into my exercise routine?

4. Sometimes I might prefer to socialize while I exercise. With whom can I share a walk or other forms of exercise?

A Long Sleep

He who keeps Israel, will neither slumber nor sleep.

Psalm 121:4

I can hardly wake up this morning, Lord. What's the matter with me? I'm not accustomed to sleeping this late. I'm acting like a teenager. Luckily, I'm retired and not required to be at work early. How did I do that?

As I look at myself in the mirror—what a sight to behold! Disheveled hair, puffy, squinting eyes. But, as I look at myself more carefully, I see that I look rested. Yippee! So, who cares that I planned to be up some time ago, or that I'm barely moving at this late hour of the morning?

Does it matter, Lord, whether or not I wake up at my appointed time? After all, I'm the one who sets the time, and I have plenty to do today but nothing that would come under the "urgent" category. Do I serve you better if I'm awake and about my morning chores early? Or, do I serve you just as well by sleeping in? Something in me says that it likely doesn't matter a bit, as long as I'm not shirking responsibilities. The main thing is that I love you, Lord, whether I'm asleep or awake, right?

Prayer

Oh, God of My Life, I know for certain that your love for me never changes—you neither slumber nor sleep. When I am awake, though, I can be aware of your love. Most importantly, I want to be awake to do the work you still want me to do in this world. It would be nice, though, if that work didn't have to start early every morning! You see, Lord, I very much enjoy the sleep that you grant me. I've had my sleepless nights, too—plenty of them—and they were no fun at all. Thank you for the gift of sleep. And thank you for never taking a break from loving me. Now, let's enjoy the day together—what's left of it! Amen.

More to Pray About

One of the spin-off benefits of retirement is the freedom to plan my own schedule—or have no schedule at all!

1. What kind of schedule (or no schedule) do I prefer?

2. Do I associate laziness with a long sleep?

3. Am I comfortable with the idea of sleeping late sometimes or am I set on a definite schedule most of the time?

4. Are there changes I want to make in my sleep habits?

Death of a Celebrity

Do not neglect to do good and to share what you have,
for such sacrifices are pleasing to God.   Hebrews 13:16

You let me live my life during this particular span of time, Lord, and I am grateful for the amazing people who are in the world during these same years. One of my favorite celebrity singers died today, and I will miss him. I enjoyed his joyful songs going 'round in my head. Please grant him a joyous homecoming to you, and reward him for sharing his talents. Had he or I been born earlier or later, I might have missed him altogether. That would have been a great loss to me!

I want to thank you, Lord, for inspiring human beings to invent amazing things like television, microphones, amplifiers, phonographs, records, tapes, CD's and all such, so that I—and everyone else—can appreciate the talents of great artists. Surely there were always notable artists alive at any given time over the centuries, but most of our ancestors didn't have the technical "gizmos" to access their gifts. With the turn of a knob I can sit in my living room and enjoy phenomenal entertainment from around the world. How fortunate! Furthermore, you have gifted me with the eyes and ears to take it all in. Thank you!

Prayer

Oh, Giver of All Talents, I thank you for the wondrous talents of others that you let me enjoy in my lifetime. I pray for artists whose energies and sacrifices provide entertainment for others to enjoy. Grant them the discipline and courage they need to communicate their gifts. May their work always praise you. I ask, too Lord, for the grace to develop my own particular talents to the best of my ability so that I may bring you glory in my own small ways, too—even in my seasoned years. Amen.

More to Pray About

Because the media bring us large doses of entertainment on a regular basis, it is easy for me to take great artists for granted, but it is a marvelous gift to be able to participate in the fruits of their talents.

1. Who are some artists that I have particularly enjoyed over the years?

2. Are there some songs, movies, plays, etc. that I would like to see or hear again soon?

3. With whom might I enjoy reminiscing about some celebrities of my generation?

Visiting a Friend

*Remember your creator in the days of your youth, before
the days of trouble come, and the years draw near when
you will say, "I have no pleasure in them."*

Ecclesiastes 12:1

I've just returned from a visit with my friend who lives in a
nursing home. She has always been a "spitfire" sort of person,
and, thankfully, she still is! I enjoyed her description of the move
from her apartment. She laughed and said, "Well, I was paying
rent anyway, and now, for an extra thousand dollars a month, I
get this little hole in the wall!" Bless her and her humor, Lord!

Listening to her, I see that ridding herself of her precious
possessions was very difficult. Obviously, her lovely black wal-
nut dining set could not fit into her 10' x 12' room which is now
her home. Her house was filled with decorative "dust catch-
ers" as she calls them, but they were the charming things that
made her house her home. She is coping with her losses and
adjusting to a scaled-down version of life.

I can learn from this friend. She is cheerful and bright-eyed
and enjoys finding humor in life, no matter what. She shows
me how to remain very much alive in spite of loss, change, and
limited surroundings. That's a lot to learn, Lord! How can I
grasp such important life lessons? How did she?

As I visit with her, I am aware of her deep faith. You have
been an important part of her life over the years. I know you

made the difference. Yes, she did her part as well, but she kept her eyes on you. I pray for that same gift, Lord, that I might stay focused on the essence of life and not get bogged down in what is insignificant.

Prayer

Oh, Lord of Many Mansions, I pray for my friend and for all who live under the care of others, and for all who are adjusting to major life changes. Give me, and all of us, the strength necessary to make adjustments gracefully so that we might grow beautiful in spite of and because of them. Keep me focused on you, Lord, as the essence of my life. Maybe then I will be able to see some good in change and be able to laugh at myself in the midst of it all. Oh, yes, I have a lot to learn, but I know you will help me! Amen.

More to Pray About

There are a number of people confined to their homes or in the care of others who might enjoy a visit now and then. I want to be a blessing to others—young, middle aged, and old—in every season of my life.

1. Who could I visit that is in need of some time and attention these days?

2. Is there someone I could invite to my home for a visit?

3. How can I bring a little cheer to someone else today?

Why?

When human beings have finished, they are just beginning, and when they stop, they are still perplexed.

Sirach 18:7

Why is this happening, Lord! The littlest guy in our family is critically ill, and everything else in the world is insignificant right now. Although I am struggling to believe in your love, Dear God, I bring him and our entire family to you. Why do such hard things happen? I am perplexed! Medications, treatments, intravenous hookups, doctors, nurses, diagnoses, prognoses, and all such are overwhelming us. Please wake me from this bad dream that consumes us, blending days and nights into a misty future.

We are in family crisis mode, and, although we're all doing our best to help, few of us know exactly what to do. We need wisdom in the midst of our tears. I realize that we have been in crisis before, . . . other painful illnesses, untimely deaths, miscarriage, accidents, a fire . . . and we made it through all those with your loving care.

But, he's so little, so special, and so ill. Why couldn't you let this happen to an older one in the family—like me, Lord? This isn't right! We who have enjoyed many seasons in this world have already partaken of your generosity. We want to see the young ones enjoy the same gifts of life. Oh, please, heal him and give him length of days to know and love you and your precious world. Oh, how I wish I could take his place.

Prayer

Oh, God of Life and Love, I place our cherished little one and our family in your hands. Gift us with your exceptional healing of the physical, emotional, and spiritual wounds of this crisis. Only your love can sustain us now. I pray that our family will grow closer to you and to each other during this difficult time, and I trust that you will bring good out of this chaos. Let me be still and know that your will has no why. Amen.

More to Pray About

No matter how long we live, the question, "Why?" plagues us without an answer.

1. When in my life did I find myself asking the question, "Why?" What answer did I come up with?

2. Are there situations these days that leave me asking the "why" question? How am I answering it?

3. How have I responded to family crises in the past? Are there particular ways that I can be helpful in the midst of family crises?

4. Can I be helpful to some other family that is currently in crisis?

SEASON OF CHANGE

"Make me open to my own life changes, Lord,
whenever they may come and
wherever they take me."

Autumn Leaves

*Hear this, O Job; stop and consider the wondrous works
of God.*   Job 37: 14

What a wonderful time of year, Lord, when you turn the leaves yellow, orange, scarlet, and gold, and I can see each tree, individually, in all its glory. A grand phenomenon you give us to enjoy every fall! Side-by-side, the trees show their separate shades and hues to make a vibrant carpet of the woods. In the height of their growing season, each tree seems to get lost (at least to my eye) among its neighbors, blending into a mass of green. Now, though, each stands out as a distinct individual. Like the leaves, we stand out from each other in looks and personalities to a greater extent as we age, too. In our youth, we tend to blend, only to become more different from each other, more colorful again, in our older age.

Surely this wonder resembles the autumn of my own life, which is all too quickly becoming late autumn, I know! It has taken me many seasons, books, and workshops to uncover the tone of my particular "pallet," the colors of my personality, the shades of who I am. I appreciate how important it is to be myself, true to my own colors, as you made me to be, Lord.

But I recognize that it is the beauty of my soul that I want to become dazzling. Shades of wisdom, compassion, and forgiveness; blends of courage and peace; tones of kindness, faithfulness, and generosity are the "colors" I seek for my soul. Without change, the leaves would not become gorgeous. And, I see that without change, I could not become distinct and colorful, either. Changes are occurring quite swiftly in my life now, but I see that, if I let them, these changes in me—as in the leaves—can embellish my finish, inside and out.

Prayer

Oh, Creator of All Beauty, thank you for the autumn splendor you give us to enjoy over and over. Your magnificence delights me. Like the trees, I want to grow more and more into a beautiful individual, capable of blending with others yet able to stand out as your separate creation. Give me the courage to always be myself, in the colors you intended. All that you made me to be, I want to be that to the fullest. And I pray, Lord, as I live on through more seasons, may my own life changes serve to season me inside and out, enhancing my beauty—body and soul! Amen.

More to Pray About

Perhaps I can spend some time outdoors and reflect on the beauty God planted in nature as well as in me. (If this isn't possible, a book or pictures of outdoor scenes will do.)

1. What are some qualities in myself that I am proud of?

2. What are the characteristics that make me stand out from others, especially as I age?

3. Are there special talents and abilities that I want to share with others in my unique way? How might I do that? When?

Mistakes

But by the grace of God I am what I am, and his grace toward me has not been in vain.   1 Corinthians 15:10

I goofed again today, Lord, and I felt foolish. I completely forgot to show up for my volunteer work! I enjoyed a leisurely morning and failed to remember that others were counting on me. It was just an absent-minded move, but it made me look irresponsible. I hate these silly things that seem to happen to me much more often lately. When I realized my mistake, I made the necessary apologies, and then I wrote this poem.

Coping with Changes

Evaporated—
that piece of peace,
present in youth,
confident, like a young pup playing,
presuming success, regardless the task.
Bewildered, instead, are graying days,
less sure, insecure,
compelling me to choose
gingerly acts, comfortable tracks;
conceal skills lost, at all cost;
prevent blatant blunder.
Persevere
despite this aging, changing self.
Endure, my dear!

Oh, Holy Spirit, please attend to me when my attention wanders and I end up doing things in muddled ways or forgetting them altogether. I don't want to lose confidence or stay home more and more just because I do ridiculous things now and then. I want, instead, to make allowances and see how human I am in my bloopers. I do have some doozies! Generally, they are not earth shattering, so I may as well have some fun with them.

Prayer

Oh, God of Fortifying Grace, I ask for courage to endure—in spite of my blunders. I know you love me, no matter what, and you are always with me, but I do need your help to keep my mind clear and focused so I don't make so many mistakes. And when I do, let me take my errors lightly and enjoy my silly moments. They bring me to you! I want to love myself in all my humanity and accept who I am today. I trust that you will grant me that grace. Thank you! Amen.

More to Pray About

People of all ages make silly mistakes, not only people who have lived many seasons! I need to remember that even when I feel like giving up on myself, God will never give up on me.

1. What can I say to myself to feel better when I have an embarrassing moment? Can I laugh at myself?

2. Are there some blunders that I could prevent? If so, how?

3. How can I pray about my mistakes when they happen?

Traveling

"I hereby command you: Be strong and courageous; do not be frightened or dismayed, for the Lord your God is with you wherever you go."   *Joshua 1:9*

I had a great time, but now I'm glad to be home! Thank you for the opportunity to see a bit more of your marvelous world, Lord. And, oh, it is splendid! But, if I do say so myself, I feel this was a gutsy thing for me to do—jump on a plane, alone, and venture off to another country! Well, I did have a friend waiting for me at my destination, so I had a built-in safety zone, and she speaks the language of the country, so I felt secure.

But, Lord, you know how my body has been lately . . . stiff and aching! And you know, too, how much my legs hurt me in the midst of museums and gardens, basilicas and boulevards. I had to keep prodding them like little donkeys that wanted to sit at every turn. But I did it! Thank you for giving me the determination necessary to accomplish what I wanted to do and the resolve to see the things that I've been waiting for years to see.

After this trip I realize how fortunate I am to have seen so many wonders; and in spite of much more to explore, my body is setting limits for how much I still can do. Somewhere down the road, I won't have the choice to travel or stay home. My limitations will determine the answer, and I'm sure I won't like the conclusion.

Prayer

Oh, Lord of the Universe, thank you for the physical stamina and financial resources I needed over the years to travel a bit in your lovely world. Now, I ask for ongoing fortitude, strength of mind and body, as I look ahead to future travel. Let me be strong and courageous; not frightened or dismayed. Give me a body and spirit that work together to praise and glorify you . . . wherever I go. Amen.

More to Pray About

Sometimes people put off traveling until their retirement only to find that they no longer have the physical stamina to travel in their later seasons.

1. Is traveling something I enjoyed early in my life? What are some good memories of early travels?

2. Can I plan to enjoy traveling during my years ahead? Where do I want to go?

3. Are there physical limitations on my travel these days? Financial limitations? Other limitations?

4. How do I feel about traveling alone? Are there groups I could travel with? Tours I might join? Where could I get useful travel information?

Shopping

. . . but those who wait for the Lord shall renew their strength, they shall mount up with wings like eagles, they shall run and not be weary, they shall walk and not faint.   *Isaiah 40:31*

I need your help, Lord! Shopping just isn't what it used to be. I get tired so easily, and the shopping I once enjoyed as a leisure experience is often a chore now. Not long ago, I could walk the halls of the malls with high energy and enthusiasm for a bargain. I miss those days, Lord! Now, by the time I get to a store or two, I have aches and pains that force me to sit a bit on those benches that must be there for people like me!

How can this be me? In my mind, I can still shop till I drop with the best of them, but my body doesn't cooperate anymore. I'm not used to this, Lord! A few purchases, and I'm ready to go to lunch. Before long, I'm happy to get home and flop down for a nap to revive my legs, feet, and back. That's not the me that I've known! I need your help to accept this new self. I don't only miss shopping, you know. I really miss the self I used to be.

Prayer

Oh, Lord of All Shoppers, my ability to roam the market-places is waning as years go by, yet, I still want to be out and about to fill my needs and enjoy my community. I pray for extra strength for myself and all of us who want to do our own shop-

ping (and have a little fun, too!). Please, give us the energy and mobility we need to get the job done and be able to enjoy it as much as possible. And, by the way, a few bargains would lighten the journey, too! Thank you, Lord. Amen.

More to Pray About

Pondering my shopping routines may give me insights into some of my current needs and concerns.

1. Have I noticed specific changes in my ability to manage my shopping chores?

2. What could I do to ease the burden of getting to and from marketplaces?

3. Is there someone who could assist me with my shopping?

4. Are there others I could help with their shopping?

Getting Ready for Bed

. . . my mouth praises you with joyful lips when I think of you on my bed, and meditate on you in the watches of the night. . .　　　　　　　　　　　　　*Psalm 63:5-6*

Amazing, Lord, how long it takes these days to get ready for a good night's sleep. Once upon a time, I could hop right into bed and dream away. But now! Wow! The "to do" list keeps growing! First, I eat a little cereal so I can fall asleep; then, floss and brush my teeth (yes, Lord, I am grateful to still have them); put lotion on my elbows and heels so the skin won't crack; drops in my eyes to prevent dryness; rub analgesic gel on my knee; say my night prayers; take my medications and lay out the pills for morning . . . no wonder I'm so tired. You know the routine, Lord! Countless preparations for the night's rest and for a new day ahead.

But my favorite part of the routine is when I review my day with you, Lord. I like to mull over the day's events, both the positive and the less-than-terrific! It is easy to be grateful for delightful moments but more difficult to accept what didn't go well or what I could have done differently. My greatest challenge, though, is to try to recognize your work in the ordinary occurrences of my life. I ask you, Lord, for the inner eyes and ears to recognize your ongoing conversation with me in the daily "stuff" of my life. I want to be able to notice how you demonstrate your love for me—routinely.

Prayer

Oh, Maker of Night and Day, as I complete one task after another to prepare for rest, make me aware that my life is always in progress, one step after another, moving me closer to you and to your plan for my eternal rest. Let me know that even the most mundane chores are important in keeping me on track toward you. May my nightly routine be a steady reminder to prepare myself for the ultimate new day when I will meet you face to face. Until then, may I rest assured of your deep love for me. And now, please grant me a restful night that will energize me to serve you and others well tomorrow. Amen, and, good night, Lord!

More to Pray About

Reviewing the day in terms of God's ongoing conversation with me is always food for reflection. So many things happen each day that unless I ponder their significance, I can lose sight of God's hand in my life.

1. As I review my nightly routine, what strikes me as humorous about what I do and how I do it?

2. Am I making night prayer a priority among my before-bed activities?

3. Does it make a difference, when I take time to review my day and reflect on God's work in my life? What do I find?

Weak Hands

. . . he said to me, "My grace is sufficient for you, for power is made perfect in weakness." So, I will boast all the more gladly of my weaknesses, so that the power of Christ may dwell in me.   2 Corinthians 12:9

I wish I could get a grip, Lord, the way I used to. These weak hands are a terrible inconvenience. At one time, I was the one to whom others would bring the tightly-sealed pickle jar and say, "Can you open this?" Confidently, I would answer, "Sure!" and my clasp did the job. My hands were strong then, and I could use them for just about anything. I yearn for those hands, Lord. I miss being able to do whatever I want without feeling pain in my thumbs, weakness in my fingers. Although the gnarled joints, brown spots, wrinkles, and scars are evidence of many life stories, I miss the strength that dwelled in my hands.

Oh, yes, Lord! Good thing you reminded me. I am grateful for what I still can do, but when I spill the milk because the jug is so heavy and I can't hang on, I feel faulty, like the unraveling rope of a collapsing swing. These little things seem to get me down, Lord. I ache for strength. Let me understand your words, about your grace being enough for me . . . your power living in me. I ask you, please, to strengthen my hands if you will, but more importantly, strengthen my spirit to adjust to these changes. Let me allow your power to work in me in spite of my weaknesses. What I need most is strong faith.

Prayer

Oh, Lord of all Power and Strength, keep me ever aware that all my strength comes from you, not from my hands nor any earthly powers. Thank you for the wonderful hands you gave me to express my life and for all the things they accomplished. Help me to continue using my hands to serve you and others in every way I can. Let me not grow tired of doing good just because I have a few weak fingers! And, when it is necessary to give these hands a little rest, let me rest them in your hands, Lord. Amen.

More to Pray About

Looking carefully at my hands can be a prayerful reflection in itself. With their lines, scars, and spots, my hands tell many life stories. My hands are a blessing and an important expression of who I am—in every season.

1. What have I accomplished with my hands for which I am grateful?

2. What do I still want to do with my hands?

3. Where in my hands do I feel weakness; where do I feel strength?

Seeing Well

Open my eyes, so that I may behold wondrous things . . .
Psalm 119:18

I notice, Lord, that lately I'm not seeing as well as I used to. Perhaps I need to have my glasses changed. I hope that's the case. But this concerns me a great deal. As you know, I've come to depend on seeing well enough to carry on my daily activities, enjoy your beauty all around me in nature, delight in my hobbies, participate in community events, see the expressions on faces when I'm visiting, and so on. I just can't imagine getting along with very poor vision, or worse yet, none at all! I know that I might have to face this though, as I look ahead at this business of aging.

As I contemplate that scenario, I am reminded of a lovely friend who became blind in her seasoned years, yet maintained a positive attitude. She told me that her loss of vision brought her a new freedom—freedom from judging others. To help me understand, she explained how she no longer can see the clothing people wear, so she doesn't make judgments about how they look. And the odd behavior of others doesn't bother her anymore because she can't see it. I remember how she laughed and expressed appreciation for being free from such things. Not that she is happy about being blind, but she discovered an unexpected benefit. She is now "blind" to negative things that occupied her over the years. Less vision brought her new freedom!

Prayer

Oh, My All-seeing God, I pray for my friend and for all who must carry on without vision, and I pray for those of us who still have sight, limited though it may be. Let me appreciate this gift, yet be prepared to manage without it. And, if it is your will that someday I must make that adjustment, let me learn both how to carry on and also how to be positive. Give me the wisdom to welcome the freedom from judgment that my friend has embraced. And, most importantly, Lord, help me to see clearly with my heart and thereby catch sight of your miracles in my life every day. Amen.

More to Pray About

What a gift my eyesight has been over the years.

1. What are some of God's greatest displays that I have been able to see and enjoy?

2. Are some of my favorite activities restricted due to failing vision now?

3. Do I fear losing my vision?

4. How do I think I would get along without my eyesight?

5. Is it time to make an appointment for an eye examination?

"Just One Today?"

"... In my Father's house there are many dwelling places .... And if I go and prepare a place for you, I will come again and will take you to myself, so that where I am, there you may be also."   *John 14:2-3*

I had a hard start at the restaurant today, Lord. The hostess was slow to seat me. Finally, she noticed me and said, "Just one today?" Oh, how that question pinched my heart. I wanted to say, "Yes. Isn't that enough?" But I held my tongue. Help me, Lord, to keep my cool in these lonely moments!

Yes, it is just one today. How I wish it were two or more, but sometimes I'm the only one I have to go out with. I realize, Lord, that this hostess never saw me laughing and talking with my friends during lunches over the years. Nor was she ever there when I came in with my loving husband, hand in hand, to order our "usuals" and enjoy each other's company. How would she know? To her I look like a lonely, little old lady no one ever took out to lunch. She doesn't know that my memories of good times are etched deeply in my heart. How would she know that one of the reasons I go there is to relish my memories.

Prayer

Oh, Lord of All Enjoyment, thank you for the good times you have given me in my life. Oh, so many! Most of the people I enjoyed during those times are no longer with me, and I dearly miss them, but my memories get me by. I pray that all people will enjoy special moments in their lives so that when they are in their seasoned years, they will have wonderful memories to "make their days," too. And, Lord, when I leave this world and enter your eternal realm, I pray that you will not be slow to seat me in the place you have prepared for me. How I long to hear you say, "Come in. You are just the one I am waiting for today." Amen.

More to Pray About

Sometimes it is difficult to go out alone, yet it may be unrealistic to expect that someone can always be at my side.

1. Where can I go by myself and still feel safe and comfortable?

2. Where am I reluctant to go because I would have to go alone?

3. Who could I invite to accompany me the next time I want to go out?

Background Music

Uh, oh! My age is showing again, Lord. Come quickly and save me from myself. I'm thinking that I need to call someone to turn down this irritating music. What kind of trouble will I get myself into, do you suppose? Do I dare open my big mouth and ask for less volume on this noise that they call background music?

When I was a bit younger, background music seemed to actually stay in the background. But now, no such luck! I simply can't hear the conversations of my companions as clearly as I once did, so the music looms large as interference. Besides, I really like soothing, melodious tunes that give me comfort rather than these jumpy, bumpy strains that strain my brain. Sorry, Lord! I'm getting carried away! I do that when I feel crazy. Please forgive me.

Okay, Lord. I'll ask to talk to the manager to see if the sound can be turned down a bit. Please help me to be charming. I'm more likely to get my way that way, right? And, if my request is turned down, maybe you can give my ears a little extra "earshot" to hear my companions in spite of the music.

What I really need, though, is for you to turn me around to be content in this place—and every place—no matter what. Please, help me to go with the flow and try to enjoy my surroundings. Give me the wisdom to know that I can't expect to always be perfectly comfortable wherever I am. Remind me that I can do all things because you give me strength! I want to turn myself over to you, no matter where I am.

Prayer

Come, Oh Great Music Maker of My Life! Bring me around from irritation to comfort—in you. Give me the strength I need right now to accept this less-than-lovely music. But, more importantly, keep me listening for your tunes everywhere in my life. I want you to be the one who plays not only the background music in my life, but the notes I listen to and the scores I live by. I pray for ears that hear; and, Lord, please give me wisdom to listen! Amen.

More to Pray About

Over the past few years, it seems that a variety of things that didn't used to irritate me, easily annoy me now. That may be due to newfound limitations—in my hearing, my vision, my strength, my movement, and so on.

1. What are some specific situations that prompt my irritations?

2. Can I attribute my annoyance to some limitation or to an attitude that I have?

3. How can I prepare myself to cope with my irritations in order to be more content?

After a Fall

Even though I walk through the darkest valley, I fear no evil; for you are with me; your rod and your staff—they comfort me.   *Psalm 23:4*

That was me on my hands and knees on the boulevard today, Lord! Oh, what a scene! My shoe caught a sidewalk crack, and I went down. The result: torn slacks, skinned knee, blood seeping here and there, and oh, so much injured pride! With the help of a passerby, I was able to rise from the occasion, get back home, and try to recover. I am grateful that all my bones are still intact, and I trust that my bruises will heal. But as you know, Lord, my emotions took a beating.

Actually, I am scared. This is not the first fall I've had in recent months. Each one brings more alarm. Apparently my sure-footedness is quickly becoming unsure. I'm concerned that if I fall again, I might not come up in one piece. I hate this feeling of insecurity. Worse yet is the vicious circle that is emerging—the less sure I am, the less confidence I have, so I'm uncomfortable and move awkwardly, and therefore I'm more likely to fall and get hurt. But I remember that even Jesus found himself fallen to the ground, so I know that you know what this feels like, Lord. Oh, how I need your help!

Prayer

My God of All Grace, you created human beings to walk on two feet, not on our hands and knees. I ask you for steadiness of body and mind so that I can move with grace and security. Please help me to be vigilant yet sure in my movements. Let me step cautiously yet optimistically forward each time I walk. Please keep me upright—in every way—as I age from day to day. Let my step-by-step movements successfully keep me from falling, but more importantly, may each stride bring me ever closer to you. Amen.

More to Pray About

Like so many things in life, falls do not only happen in later seasons. However, recovering from falls becomes more challenging over the years; thus, greater concern.

1. Am I prone to falling?

2. Under what conditions do my movements sometimes result in a fall?

3. Do I need to discuss a fall or falls with my doctor? or with someone else?

4. Is there something I can do to feel more safe?

X-Rays

Dear friend, I pray that all may go well with you and that you may be in good health, just as it is well with your soul.   *3 John:2*

Bone on bone! No padding left in some joints, Lord. The X-Rays saw what I have been feeling. No wonder I have pain! But that's not the end of it. The prognosis is: "more deterioration expected." I'm not doing well with this information, but I surely cannot change it, so here I am, contemplating impending infirmity, and that brings me straight to you, Lord.

Although the doctor ordered medication and is sending me to learn some helpful exercises, I'm left with the reality that my body is slowly but surely declining. I am grieving this loss. But Dear Jesus, I believe you know my grief, and you are with me. I understand that living longer is bound to bring losses. Until recently, though, they were developments that I heard other people discussing. At this point, they are becoming my own. This is a difficult challenge for me, Lord!

Prayer

Dear God, Designer of My Life, I come to you asking for X-Ray eyes to see opportunities to intensify my faith. May my physical infirmity strengthen me spiritually. Lead me to grow inwardly more whole in spite of my body's decline and eventual death. I am determined to remain as fully alive as possible—physically, mentally, emotionally, socially and spiritually—for as long as possible. Yet, realistically, I know that I won't get out of this world alive! So, I want my body's course to draw me closer to you. Keep me focused on my eventual return to you, Lord. And, until that time, give me the heartiness I need to meet my daily challenges. Let me accept your plan calmly and without fear because I know you are always with me! One day at a time—with you—will be my motto! Amen.

More to Pray About

No matter how much I try to take care of myself, I will experience changes due to aging.

1. What specific anomalies have surfaced for me recently?

2. How am I responding to these changes?

3. Is there someone with whom I can visit about these things?

4. Is there someone else experiencing similar changes to whom I could offer support?

A "Close Call"

God is our refuge and strength, a very present help in
trouble.   *Psalm 46:1*

Home, safe and sound after all, Lord! I wondered there for a while. Surely you know that I nearly had a "fender bender" today. I'm still shook up about it. Pulling into that intersection seemed safe and clear, but another car came speeding at me from out of nowhere; and, quick as a blink—a near miss! Gratefully, the other driver gave me a little grace (and a little horn) and slowed down while I maneuvered as needed. Gave me a scare, though, to say the least!

So, here I am, Lord, humbly handing myself over to you for comfort and care. I always considered myself a good driver, or at least adequate; but after today, I may not feel confident enough to get behind the wheel again. I was just happy to get myself home. That near miss took a lot of steam out of my inner engine. Whether that's good or bad is not clear to me at this point. Are my driving skills diminishing? Or, is this just a reality check that will make me a better driver in the future. I don't want to be a road hazard, nor do I want to depend on someone else every time I want to go out. This is not easy, Lord. I truly need your direction.

Prayer

Oh, Lord of All Movement, I pray that you will teach me how all roads can lead to you if I let them. I realize that I might be at a crossroads regarding my own transportation. Let me carefully and realistically evaluate the significance of today's close call. Help me to take an honest look at my driving skills, and give me courage to act in the best interest of myself and others. Regardless the path this takes, let me find you along the way, Lord. I trust you are with me in this matter—as you are in every other one. Amen.

More to Pray About

This is not the only time in my life that I had a close call on the road; but in these seasoned years, I question myself in a new way. Such questioning can be useful as long as I am honest with myself and make adjustments as needed.

1. Is my current mode of transportation working well for me or are some changes in order?

2. How would I manage to get around if I could no longer drive a car?

3. With whom can I discuss my driving in order to get an objective viewpoint as well as some direction?

Feeling Left Out

No one shall be able to stand up against you all the days of your life. As I was with Moses, so I will be with you; I will not fail you or forsake you.   Joshua 1:5

"Out to pasture." "Time for new blood." "Moving on!" There are many terms for it, Lord, but I'm feeling left out, no matter what I call it. A group I used to enjoy is gathering without me today. This time I wasn't asked to take part. Evidently, I've been given my walking papers without even receiving the usual pink slip. I feel like an ugly duckling kicked out of the nest. What did I do? What didn't I do? Do they think I am just too old for them now?

It must be common for people my age to feel they just don't fit in anymore, for one reason or another. I don't want to admit that. And, more importantly, I wish I could make the decision about fitting in or not rather than having the decision made for me. Disengagement, I think they call this!

It seems to me that disengagement might be just fine when both the "disengagee" and the "disengager" come to a friendly understanding about it. Right now, I'm a reluctant disengagee, and I need your help to get through this, Lord.

My aging process continues to be a challenge for me. I admit that being left out of my little group is, overall, a small loss, but it stings me nonetheless. Help me to make lemonade out of yet another lemon. Pretty large pitcher already, I'd say! Finding enough "sugar" to add is the hard part! So, I pray to be sweet about this loss and see it as a reminder of the bigger losses, and ultimately, the big one!

Prayer

Oh, Lord of All Connections, keep me engaged in things that matter. Not everything I have been a part of is essential to my well being, so when I must disengage or am disengaged from something, I pray to bow out gracefully. I believe that you will never disengage me from your endless love.And, that's the group I want to be in, Lord! Secure me there, always, where I know I will never feel left out. Meanwhile, show me where I can feel secure here as well—at least as much as is possible in this world. Amen.

More to Pray About

Throughout my lifetime, I found my place in various groups, or at least I tried to. Now, in my seasoned years, some of those groups still fit me, others may not. Perhaps some new associations could be better for me than my former ones.

1. In which groups am I most comfortable these days?

2. Which groups do I want to let go?

3. Is there a new group that I would enjoy? How could I become part of it?

4. Is there someone else that I might invite to be part of a group that I belong to?

Feeling "Invisible"

*. . . we look not at what can be seen but at what cannot
be seen; . . . for what cannot be seen is eternal.*

2 Corinthians 4:18

It happened at the optical shop today, Lord. I felt invisible. My feeling frightened me, so when I came home, I wrote this poem. Then I prayed again.

> Do You See Me?
> How long will it be
> before you notice me?
> Do you think I don't care?
> Perhaps my hair gives you a scare.
> My round body makes you shrink?
> These wrinkles cause a blink?
> If I were blond in thigh-high skirt,
> you might perceive I have some worth.
> But, now I wait; I go on by,
> unnoticed by your blinded eye.
> I wish I could prescribe for you
> new glasses with a sharpened view
> that bring to focus those you hold
> invisible because we're old.
> You don't know what you're missing!

When did it start, Lord, my being ignored? This experience of being overlooked? It happened so slowly that I didn't see it coming. When I was young and dressed in suits and heels, I seemed to command attention when I needed or wanted it. Now, I have the same needs, but others don't notice. That hurts!

Help me, My Understanding Lord, to be tolerant of others and what seems to be their fear of aging. Maybe they see themselves —in the future—when they see my gray hair and wrinkles. Perhaps they think if they ignore me, it won't happen to them. But, someday, they will know!

Prayer

Oh, My God of All Ages, thank you for loving me regardless of my age, my size, shape, hair color, and wrinkles. Thank you for seeing the real me, inside and out. I pray for all those who, like me, feel invisible. Let us know that it is most important to be visible to you. And, please Lord, help those who serve people who have lived many seasons to see us as the real people we are. May they treat us the way they would like to be treated when they are well seasoned. Amen.

More to Pray About

People who have lived long are not the only ones to ever feel "invisible." Certainly children are easily ignored; so are people who have disabling conditions.

1. Have I been responsible for ignoring other people from time to time, giving them that "invisible" feeling? How do I feel when that happens to me?

2. Is there something I can do to prevent that feeling—for myself? for others?

Life Soup

. . . he took the seven loaves and the fish; and after giving thanks he broke them and gave them to the disciples, and the disciples gave them to the crowds. And all of them ate and were filled; and they took up the broken pieces left over, seven baskets full.

Matthew 15:36-37

Impressed with what I can do with a few leftovers, a little broth, and a handful of noodles, I stir a little, and there it is—soup! Pretty neat, don't you think, Lord? Oh, it's just a lowly batch of soup—nothing like what you did to feed the crowds, but I feel proud when my leftovers turn into delicious soup.

Here I am, stirring this nourishment of assorted parts, thinking about leftovers and about how many of them I have in my life. Oh, no Lord, I don't mean the kind I store in the refrigerator. I mean the leftovers, the broken pieces that I store in my heart. Things such as . . . hopes and dreams, projects that I started and stopped, good ideas that I never shared with anyone, people that I loved but had to leave behind, places I visited and would like to return to . . . and so the list goes on.

As I age, Lord, I'm beginning to realize that there will never be enough time for me to get everything done to neatly complete the fragments of myself. The life that I lived has become its own batch of soup, made up of my relationships, my work at home and away, my faith, goals I achieved, the good and the bad that I did, my joys, pains, sufferings, and all such. But still, it seems there could be yet another batch of life soup, made from the pieces that didn't make it to the serving bowl of my life, so they remain my still-want-tos, I-wish-I-could-haves, and yet-to-be-accomplished.

Oh, don't get me wrong, Lord. I'm not complaining, nor do I feel discouraged to have these life leftovers which eventually I'll have to leave behind. After all, the possibilities in life seem to be infinite, so how could I experience everything in one lifetime? That's what eternity is for, right? I believe that I will find a completion of myself blended there with all the rest of humanity. Now that will be a motley brew!

Prayer

Oh, My Loving Lord, I am grateful for the fabulous ingredients of life that you have already given me to experience, and I give you the array of possibilities that I simply could not squeeze into my lifetime. I bring you my life leftovers to stir into an eternal mix of glory, as only you can. I look forward to ongoing potential as I anticipate my remaining days and my life hereafter. And, Dear God of All That Is Delicious, I won't be surprised to find that you have saved a spectacular array of specialties that you just couldn't give us in this world. We'll need to see you in order to fathom their wonder. Yes, I'll bet you are cooking up quite a batch of marvels to share with us in eternity. I await your treats. Soup, maybe! Amen.

More to Pray About

There is no time like the present to look after the affairs of my life, of my faith, and of my heart.

1. What hopes and dreams do I still want to accomplish in my life?

2. Are there people I want to visit whom I have not seen for a while?

3. Do I have any regrets that I can try to reverse?

4. Do I have some unfinished business in my life that I need to look after?

5. Are there specific people who can help me take care of any "leftovers" that are in my

Spider's Pearls

Joanne Ardolf Decker

12/88

"Work your work in me so that I become
a piece of beautiful art during this season of my life."